ORGANIZING KNOWLEDGE

THEN AND NOW

ORGANIZING KNOWLEDGE
THEN AND NOW

Edited by
B.K. Sen
Chairman, Bibliometric Experts' Committee,
Dept. of Science and Technology,
Govt. of India

Bidyarthi Dutta
Asst. Professor,
Dept. of Library & Information Science
Vidyasagar University, Midnapore,
West Bengal - 721102

Ess Ess Publications
New Delhi

ORGANIZING KNOWLEDGE
Then and Now

ISBN: 978-81-7000-748-7

First Published 2015

Published by:
Ess Ess Publications
4831/24, Ansari Road,
Darya Ganj,
New Delhi-110 002.
INDIA
Phones: 23260807, 41563444
Fax: 41563334
E-mail: info@essessreference.com
www.essessreference.com

Cover Design by *Patch Creative Unit*

Printed and bound in India at Salasar Imaging Systems.

Dedicated to
My Respected Teacher
&
Beloved Guide
MRS. ARUNA KARANJAI
(1946-2008)

CONTENTS

ACKNOWLEDGEMENTS

I take this opportunity to express gratitude and thanks from the core of my heart to those without whose co-operation this book would not have seen the light of the day. I want to express profuse thanks to Ms. Smita Sett, Dr. Pijush Kanti Jana, and Durga Sankar Rath, all from the Department of Library & Information Science, Vidyasagar University, Midnapore, West Bengal, for their non-stop inspiration and cordial co-operation in helping me complete this book. The inspiration and co-operation from my beloved junior colleagues, viz. Dr. Nivedita Bhattacharyya Sahoo, Dr. Soumen Mallick and Mrs. Snigdha Naskar is also thankfully acknowledged. The assistance from Mr. Biswanath Tudu and Mr. Ratan Mahato is gratefully acknowledged. The co-operation from Dr. Anup Kumar Das, Documentation Offices, CSSP, Jawaharlal Nehru University, New Delhi is also gratefully acknowledged.

I'm indebted to my respected teachers Dr. Bimal Kanti Sen, Dr. Krishnapada Majumder, Dr. Chaitali Dutta for some valuable suggestions and remarks.

The co-operation from my family members deserves special mention. Inspiration from my father, Prof. Ranajit Kr. Dutta, resulted in a quick turnover of this assignment. Bhaswati constantly maintained rhythm, and last but not the least, sweet interruptions from my little "Khushi" added flavor to this project.

- Bidyarthi Dutta

PREFACE

"Knowledge has to be improved, challenged and increased constantly, or it vanishes", Said Peter Drucker, the celebrated management scientist. Information is considered as a strategic resource in the present-day society. Knowledge is the derivative of information as information is the derivative of data. A key factor is innate within this transitional process, i.e. organization. Data becomes information only when it is organized, otherwise it would be the lump of figures. Similarly information becomes knowledge when it is placed in actionable context. Without context, information bears no value. David Jones remarked that, "In the world of knowledgeable management, Data is ubiquitous, Information is contextuous and Knowledge is illustrious.....". Knowledge organization is thus the key factor in all areas of explorations of human intellect and talent. Once organized the knowledge would be disseminated more swiftly to pave the way for further budding of new bits of information that in turn would create further knowledge. This is a recursion process that makes knowledge generation and dissemination process height faster today. "The saddest aspect of life right now is that science gathers knowledge faster than society gathers wisdom", remarked Issac Asimov. The concept of knowledge organization is almost contemporary to the concept of knowledge in the society. It was incepted by

Aristotle around 350 B.C. The mode of knowledge organization has been continuously changing with time. Today this change has become very dynamic and faster. This book attempts to briefly chalk out the entire course of knowledge organization and the major changing features with time.

This book covers major facets of knowledge organization in thirteen chapters. The first chapter gives the brief introduction. The second chapter provides an outline of knowledge society, particularly in the context of functions and activities of UNESCO. The third chapter describes the traditional ways of knowledge organization. The fourth chapter describes the modern views of knowledge organization. The views of Birger Hjorland are described particularly with details. The fifth chapter enumerates different categories of information from different contexts. The sixth chapter describes the concepts of information explosion and information overloading. Several psychological impacts of information overloading are described. The seventh chapter lists the possible ways of control of information. The eighth chapter describes the role and functions of keywords as fundamental building block of information and the ninth chapter states different categories of the keywords with examples. The tenth chapter introduces the basic concepts of folksonomy and tagging. The eleventh and twelfth chapters discuss the basic concepts of domain ontology and semantic web respectively. The thirteenth and the last chapter describes the concepts of Web 2.0 and Library 2.0 with examples.

It is hoped that this book will be helpful to the students and researchers of Library and Information science.

- Bidyarthi Dutta

1
Introduction

The sphere of "Knowledge" covers the entire universe. Knowledge is originated from the process of thinking governed by human mind. Mind is a reservoir in which intellectual work is stored. When man's intellect entangles his wisdom to reflect some new light from mind, it is called idea or thinking. Thinking is a continuous process, which results in knowledge explosion. The process of "Classification" starts with knowledge. If there is no knowledge, there is no classification. The purpose of classification is to bring related items together in a helpful sequence from general to the specific. The process of classification of universe of knowledge may be encountered from two different approaches, e.g. enumerative classification and faceted classification. An enumerative classification attempts to assign tags for all the single and composite subject concepts required in the system. Enumerative classification is hierarchical in nature. A hierarchical classification is essentially based on the assumption that the process of subdivision and collocation would display in a comprehensive way the maximum possible number of components of the subject concerned, proceeding from classes to divisions; and from divisions to subdivisions in a logical way. Thus all simple, compound and complex subjects are listed in the schedules of an enumerative classification scheme. The enumerative classification delves the universe of knowledge more and more to explore all possible subsets exist in the long spectrum of subject. The faceted classification, on the contrary, doesn't rely on the breakdown of a universe of subjects but on building up from the subject statements of particular documents. Faceted classification is based on the definition of a facet. A facet is the sum-total of the isolates formed by the division of a subject by one characteristic of division. An isolate is an idea or idea complex fit to form a component of a subject, but it doesn't by itself constitute a subject. Thus "Child" is an isolate. It is fit to be a component of such subjects as "Education of child" or "Psychology of child". In faceted classification the subject statements are analysed into their component elemental concepts, which are known as isolates. These isolates are listed in the schedules. A faceted classification thus doesn't assign fixed slots to subjects in sequence, but uses clearly defined, mutually exclusive, and collectively exhaustive aspects, properties or characteristics of a class or specific subject. The subjects are analysed at first into isolates, and then synthesized to form different classes; for this reason a faceted classification is known as analytico-synthetic classification. Most traditional classification systems are basically hierarchical and enumerative. But the more recent schemes tend to be faceted.

Classification of knowledge has a long history. The earliest known system of classification was framed by Aristotle (384 B.C to 322 B.C). He attempted in the 4th century B.C. to group animals according to some specific criteria, e.g. mode of reproduction and possession or lack of red blood. Aristotle's pupil Theophrastus classified plants according to their uses and methods of cultivation. Little interest was shown in classification until the 17th and 18th century, when botanists and zoologists began to devise the modern scheme of categories. Before the idea of evolution there was no impetus to show more meaningful relationships among species. The concept of knowledge organization forms the central theme of classification of knowledge.

Francis Bacon's (1561-1626) system classified materials as functions of the three basic faculties: history (natural, civil, literary, ecclesiastical) as the function of memory; philosophy (including theology) as that of reason; and poetry, fables, and the like as that of imagination.

August Comte (1798-1857) formulated a distinctive theory of the way in which knowledge developed historically and of the relationship between its branches. He regarded philosophy as the co-ordination of all the sciences. His classification consists of only six fundamental sciences: mathematics, astronomy, physics, chemistry, biology and sociology. Comte's theory of classification contains a distinctive philosophical viewpoint, which is known as positivism.

Around 1900, Charles A. Cutter (1837-1903), Ernest Cushing Richardson (1860-1939), William Charles Berwick Sayers (1881-1960) and Henry Evelyn Bliss (1870-1955) strongly emphasized that the classification of books in libraries is basically governed by the organization of knowledge, as represented in the documents of the library. The origin of the phrase knowledge organization in LIS is clearly related to their works, according to which book classification is basically knowledge organization and the knowledge needed to classify books comes from knowledge production, of which the books are the tangible expression.

According to C. A. Cutter: "I believe . . . that the maker of a scheme for book arrangement is the most likely to produce a work of permanent value, if he keeps always before his mind a classification of knowledge" (Cutter, 1889). The Expansive Classification system, which was introduced by Charles A. Cutter, was developed in seven stages: the first, being very simple, for the smallest library, and, finally, the seventh, designed for the largest library (Cutter, 1904). Each level was of increasing complexity. Cutter's aim was to prepare a scheme applicable to collections of every size, from the village library in its earliest stages to the national library with a million volumes. As the library is a growing organism, each section of the classification would be further sub-divided and increased in specificity.

Sayers expressed the idea in the following way: "A book classification must hold the minuteness of the knowledge classification as an ideal to which it must approximate as nearly as possible" and "It must be clearly borne in mind, however, that the classification of knowledge should be the basis of the classification of books; that the latter obeys in general the same laws, follows the same sequence". (Sayers, 1915)

Richardson said: "In general the closer a classification can get to the true order of the sciences and the closer it can keep to it, the better the system will be and the longer it will last". (Richardson, 1964)

Bliss asserts that "Knowledge should be organized in consistency with the scientific and educational consensus, which is relatively stable and tends to become more so as theory and system become more definitely and permanently in general and increasingly in detail." According to him the order of the subjects should be the prime concern of any library (Bliss, 1935). He devised Bibliographic Classification System, which was published in four volumes between 1940 and 1953.

James Duff Brown's theory of subject classification followed the order of scientific progression, in which matter and force came first, which gave rise to life, and life was followed by mind. Finally mind was followed by the making of its record.

In 1876, Melvil Dewey (1851-1931) devised an elegant method for categorizing the books on all subjects. The Dewey Decimal System divides books into 10 broad subject areas and several hundred sub-areas and then assigns each volume a precise number, for instance, 025.3 for any document on Library Classification Theory. But on the Internet, a new approach to categorization is currently emerging. Thomas Vander Wal, an information architect and Internet developer, has called it folksonomy, i.e. the folk taxonomy or people's taxonomy.

In 1873, Amherst College student Melvil Dewey presented a proposal to the faculty for re-organizing the college library collection. He worked in the college library and was frustrated by the lack of logic in the way the books were shelved. Dewey pondered the problem until he suddenly thought of using decimals to create a simple, standardized system for cataloging and arranging libraries. The faculty was so impressed with Dewey's plan that they let him reorganize the library's holdings. After graduation, he was appointed as Acting Librarian. In 1876 he published a pamphlet about his method, and libraries all over the country soon adopted what has been known ever since as the Dewey Decimal Classification System. At present, this is the most popular classification scheme through the world.

Another famous scheme is Universal Decimal Classification (UDC), which was developed by the *Belgian* bibliographers Paul Otlet and Henri la Fontaine at the end of the 19th century. It is based on the Dewey Decimal Classification, but uses auxiliary signs to indicate various special aspects of a subject and relationships between subjects. It thus contains a significant faceted or analytico-synthetic element, and is used in special libraries. UDC has been modified and extended over many years to cope with the increasing output in all disciplines of human knowledge, and is still under continuous review to take account of new developments.

Herbert Putnam (1861-1955) developed Library of Congress Classification (LCC) system in 1897. It is used by most research and academic libraries in the U.S. and several other countries. This scheme was influenced by Cutter Expansive Classification, and the DDC. Although it divides subjects into broad categories, it is essentially enumerative in nature. It provides a guide to the books housed in the library, but it has limitations to become an internationally accepted classification scheme.

S. R. Ranganathan (1892-1972) developed Colon classification (CC) system, which was the first ever faceted (or analytico-synthetic) classification. The first edition was published in 1933. Since then six more editions have been published. It is especially used in some libraries in India. Its name "Colon classification" comes from the use of colons to separate facets in class numbers. This classification scheme uses 42 main classes that are combined with other letters and numbers.

Bartol Brinkler (1916-1993) developed Brinkler Classification system in 1960, which was based on the geographical aspect of a subject. Brinkler explored varieties of subject headings and tested their usefulness to an information clientele. He found that the usefulness of a subject-heading to an information clientele depends on the level of familiarity of him with the concerned topic and what approach he/she would take when searching for resources on that topic. Generally information seekers look for everything on a particular topic, or everything regarding a particular place. Bartol Brinkler investigated a system of classification that will best serve these two types of clientele.

The general classification systems have been discussed so far, and besides, so many special classification schemes exist. In India, the Classification Research Group (CRG) was established by S. R. Ranganathan, M. A. Gopinath, A. Neelameghan et al at Documentation Research and Training Centre (DRTC),

Bangalore in 1962 to develop special classification schemes on various subjects from natural science. Profuse number of special classification schemes on diverse areas of knowledge exists today.

The DDC and UDC are more than 100 years old, and both are still widely used and constantly updated, yet in practice some major problems in using them exist. The notable feature is that, no classification scheme has been regarded as fully complete and perfectly accurate. As the universe of knowledge is continuously expanding, therefore new ideas are constantly evolving and new subjects are consequently created. It is not possible for any scheme to provide absolutely all possible subjects in the schedule. Therefore, inadequacies always remain in all classification schemes. Every new idea in the field of knowledge classification may be regarded as a new bud, which will blossom into a new flower in the next dawn to divulge some new colour resembling another fresh bit of knowledge. Such new colours make some new ways of knowledge evolution. Such ways are essentially different from those represented by the established systems of 100 years old. U. Miller said, "The 'Library of Congress Subject Headings' was a nineteenth century solution to nineteenth-century problems. It is time to fundamentally rethink our approach to the whole issue of knowledge-management and controlled-vocabulary access systems and apply that new thinking to provide access to the Web". This is the situation what we are facing today. The existing classification schemes were meant for arrangement of books on the shelves. Today we are more conversant with web resources than printed books. As all the existing schemes are nearly or more than 100 years old, they are silent about the web resources. All classification systems deal with subjects formed from universe of knowledge. A subject is developed by clustering some concepts and any concept or ides is fundamentally represented by one or a set of keywords. The keyword thus comprises the fundamental building block of a subject, which gives the content-information. A keyword may thus be looked upon as the fundamental quanta of information of a subject. The selection of appropriate keywords from a subject is a logical function. Determination of the demarcation line between a subject and its keyword is another crucial task. Today's subject will become tomorrow's keyword. For instance, the word "Artificial Intelligence" was just a keyword and existed within the domain of the subject computer science only a decade ago, but today it is regarded as a full-fledged subject. There is an ongoing trend of continuous changing of phase of the terms. The keywords acquire broader contexts and transformed to the domain of a broad subject. The existing classification schemes are silent about such dynamism of keywords. They are unable to trace the demarcation line between a subject and a keyword. The frequency of updating is not also adequate. That's why the latest edition of DDC schedule doesn't contain the keywords like Globalization, Proteome, Web 2.0, Folksonomy... and many more; which are very popular keywords today.

Increase in precision is the greatest challenge for today's information retrieval performance. Recall ratio is quite good for almost all search engines, i.e. there is no miss, but poor precision accounts for a high quantity of noise. Reduction in noise is possible only if the correct and pin-pointed keyword is chosen for searching. An up-to-date subject access tool, in today's poor precisional information retrieval scenario, should be based on association among the keywords to build up a subject, but not on dividing a broad subject into narrower compartments. Today we have so many search engines, which have very high recall ratio; but the main problem lies in precision ratio. A single keyword results in millions of hits, of which almost 99.99% is quite irrelevant. One of the major causes of poor precision is ignorance about pertinent keyword of both the information professional and information clientele. In most of the situations the proper keyword can not be selected and confusion arises due to overloading of keywords. The existing subject access tools like, list of subject headings (LCSH and Sear's list), classification schedules and various thesauri tell us the names of the keywords only and their broader and narrower terms. But these subject access tools never analyse weightage of a keyword or relevance of a keyword in the context of a particular research area. The existing subject access tools do not tell about the properties of a keyword. By exploring any such tool one can mere know what keywords exist related to any subject, but it is not possible to get any information that whether those keywords are stable or ephemeral in that subject. The high potential keyword clusters point out promising areas of research while obsolete keywords indicate waning areas.

This is the high time to remodel classification system in terms of keywords. We have so long considered document classification only, but now we need information classification. The document classification is governed by subject heading, as a document reflects an essence of a subject(s). The information classification, on the other hand, is governed by keyword, as a bit of information can be represented by a keyword(s). Traditional classification systems are enumerative and follow hierarchical taxonomic pattern. A hierarchical taxonomy is a top-down approach. In contrast to *taxonomy*, another recent trend of classification spread through the cyber world, which is known as *folksonomy*. Folksonomy is a classification system that uses a crowd of terms rather than delving single subject. The idea of a folksonomy is closely related to tagging, which has enjoyed great vogue in online circles since 2006 at least. The word "*Folksonomy*" is a combination of "*Folks*", meaning "people", and "*-onomy*", meaning "management". Literally, this means "management by people". The information clientele decide their own keywords and tag. This is the crux theme lying behind the concept of folksonomy. As information clientele or information seeker people are involved in developing keywords, the term "Folksonomy" is also defined as "Folk-Taxonomy". The two terms "Folk" and "Taxonomy" have been fused into a single word "Folksonomy". In contrast to the top-down approach of taxonomy, the folksonomy follows bottom-up approach. Folksonomy is criticized because its lack of terminological control, which causes unreliable and inconsistent keywords. If tags are freely chosen instead of taking from a given vocabulary, synonyms (multiple tags for the same concept), homonyms (same tag used with different meaning), and polysemy (same tag with multiple related meanings) are likely to arise, lowering the efficiency of content indexing and searching. As merits and demerits always co-exist in any system, folksonomy is gaining large popularity in spite of lack of standardizations of keywords. The voyage from hierarchical taxonomy to user-generated folksonomy has a very long history. Some important milestones on the way are Industrial Revolution, Second World War and Information Revolution started at late nineties. Second World War is an epoch-making landmark in the records of historical events of the last century. The industrial society gradually turned into information-based society since the end of this war. Data and information were the main driving force of this society. Another new era prevailed over the information-based society to take a new turn towards the post-modern society since late eighties of the last century, which is utterly knowledge-based. It is knowledge, which is the main driving force of this post-modern, post-information-based society. Before switching over to changing trends of information processing and organisation in the context of new modes of classification, let's have a quick look through the knowledge-based society.

2
Knowledge Society

The ancient civilization was sustained on agro-based society, where plough and soil were the main driving forces. The industrial revolution formed an industry-based society, where machinery was the main driving force behind all planning and implementations. The onward trend of industry-base remained persistent upto the end of First World War, and gradually changed orientations towards information-base since the beginning of Second World War, which is an epoch-making landmark in the records of historical events of the last century. The data and information were the main driving force of the information-based society. Today we are living in an age of change unparalleled in history. Technological, cultural and social upheavals have impacted us with regularity and increasing ferocity, radically changing the way we live, work and learn. In particular, these changes have been all pervasive in fields like education, research and industry. The traditional frameworks of learning, research and development are being challenged by technological innovation. The academic system is continuously changing. The libraries are also undergoing through so many evolutionary changes like digital library and virtual library etc from the traditional close-walled book-store concept. The traditional library system today can hardly fulfill the needs of the students, faculty members, research scholars and scientists. Both the information need and information seeking behaviour are also considerably changed. Information professionals need to know more than just their subject to serve information clientele. They need to know the ways to be properly informed, the ways not to be misinformed; they need to know how individuals experience their information need. In traditional learning system several students gather together into a lecture room to sit for some hours to listen to lectures and after that they visit library to collect some notes from some recommended text books. Some time later they are required to restate the information they have copied onto paper in a manner that is pleasing to the examiners. If they keep to the rules they earn a pass mark. This is the prevalent model of higher education and traditional library system, which are evidently inadequate to meet many of the needs of the contemporary information society. In spite of so many initiatives, antiquated practices are still very much in evidence, underlining the fact that generally the traditional learning system is not moving with the times. The traditional library cannot survive in its present format, because global trends are ensuring that alternative methods are gaining ground. The traditional library and information system mainly deal with macroscopic documents, which include both book and non-book material in print format. Today libraries are developing collections in electronic media in various formats like CD-ROM, online database, online e-journal consortia etc. The transition from print to electronic media caused a drastic change to the present-day library scenario. But, still the macroscopic documents are the main concern of the electronic media. Information professionals and clientele always look for book, journal-article, conference-proceedings etc. through different search parameters like author, title, subject, publisher, call no. etc. along with the electronic media. Traditional systems co-existing with electronic system are known as hybrid library and information systems. Such hybrid systems are highly convenient for today's information seekers in the context of their changed information need.

As new information and communication technologies brought major impact on all aspects of life, UNESCO took major initiatives to increase information and computer literacy among general public throughout the globe. None can sustain properly in today's information society without having information literacy at a certain level. This situation impelled UNESCO to keep people aware with the new ethical, legal and societal challenges by establishing a permanent international monitoring mechanism in November 1997. UNESCO introduced an Information Society Observatory to monitor the development of the information society towards knowledge society. In October 1998, the first framework of this Observatory was presented during the second international congress on Info-ethics, held in Monaco. The basic purpose of the observatory was to provide updated information in the context of the following issues in different parts of the world:

- Access to information in public domain,
- E-commerce,
- Privacy and confidentiality in cyberspace,
- Violence in cyberspace.

The UNESCO online Observatory is a dynamic entity and it developed an Internet-based gateway to online resources on ethical, legal, socio-cultural and policy issues of the Information Society. The current UNESCO mandate commits the Observatory to pay due attention to the impact of globalization on knowledge societies through the collection of pertinent information and monitoring of main trends. As a part of UNESCO's strategy to build knowledge societies, the Observatory monitors the development of knowledge societies through the following activities:

- Recognizing, assembling and arranging relevant, high-quality and multilingual information on the evolution of ethical, legal, socio-cultural and policy issues of the Information Society at the regional, national and international levels, with particular attention to education, science, culture and communication;
- Providing timeliness of information;
- Covering broad international developments and events;
- Sharing information about the challenges of the Information Society and advances in ICT;
- Providing a joint platform for UNESCO's clearing houses related to the Information Society issues (including ICT in Education Portal, Free Software Portal, Multilingualism in Cyberspace website, UNESCO WSIS Action Directory, IFAP Projects data base, IFAP Best Practices data base);
- Creating a network of users and content providers and interacting with them through community tools;
- Serving as a best practice for other organizations working in the area of the Information Society.

WORLD SUMMIT ON THE INFORMATION SOCIETY: A UN ENDEAVOUR

The World Summit on the Information Society (WSIS) was a pair of United Nations-sponsored conferences about information, communication and the information society that took place in 2003 in Geneva and in 2005 in Tunis. One of its chief objectives was to bridge the global digital divide separating rich countries from poor countries by spreading access to the Internet in the developing world. The conferences established 17 May as World Information Society Day.

The UN General Assembly endorsed the holding of the World Summit on the Information Society (WSIS) in two phases. The first phase took place in Geneva from 10 to 12 December 2003 and the second phase took place in Tunis, from 16 to 18 November 2005.

Geneva Phase: 10-12 December 2003

The objective of the first phase was to develop a statement of political will and take concrete steps to establish the foundations for an Information Society for all, reflecting all the different interests at stake. Nearly 50 Heads of state/government and Vice-Presidents, 82 Ministers, and 26 Vice-Ministers from 175 countries as well as high-level representatives from international organizations, private sector, and civil society attended the Geneva Phase of WSIS and gave political support to the Geneva Declaration of Principles and Geneva Plan of Action that were adopted on 12 December 2003. More than 11,000 participants from 175 countries attended the Summit and related events.

Tunis Phase: 16-18 November 2005

The objective of the second phase was to put Geneva's Plan of Action into motion as well as to find solutions and reach agreements in the fields of Internet governance, financing mechanisms, and follow-up and implementation of the Geneva and Tunis documents. Nearly 50 Heads of state/government and Vice-Presidents and 197 Ministers, Vice Ministers and Deputy Ministers from 174 countries as well as high-level representatives from international organizations, private sector, and civil society attended the Tunis Phase of WSIS and gave political support to the Tunis Commitment and Tunis Agenda for the Information Society that were adopted on 18 November 2005. More than 19,000 participants from

174 countries attended the Summit and related events.

The central theme of WSIS is information for all, irrespective of caste, class, creed, ethnicity and nationality. The voice of information society asserts the promise of information for all, whereas at the same time, the digital divide creates barrier between info-rich and info-poor groups, effectively opening up channels of information for privileged class only. UNESCO has taken up various initiatives to smash such barriers. The other notable attempt is Information For All Programme (IFAP), an inter-governmental programme of UNESCO. The IFAP is the only intergovernmental programme exclusively dedicated to promoting universal access to information and knowledge for development. This is a key plank in building Knowledge Societies. This programme also set up the Intergovernmental Council for the IFAP to create awareness about issues pertaining to the use of information and ICT for development at the international level. One of the prime objectives of IFAP is to measure information literacy, which refers to an integrated set of skills essential for people in all aspects of their lives. As derived from the Alexandria Proclamation of 2005, information literacy is the capacity of people to:

- Recognize their information needs;
- Locate and evaluate the quality of information;
- Store and retrieve information;
- Make effective and ethical use of information, and
- Apply information to create and communicate knowledge.

The development of indicators of information literacy is important at both national and international levels. Information literacy points out many of the purposes, for instance, combating diseases and enhancing employment opportunities. Indicators of information literacy can help different nations to identify the effect of policies to promote information literacy development and to know the extent to which their members are able to participate in a knowledge society. This is why UNESCO, through its Information for All Programme, decided to engage in the development of an international framework for measuring information literacy through which achievements at both international and national levels can be demonstrated and future efforts can be better focused.

The supporting platform of WSIS, the Internet Governance Forum (IGF), has been established by United Nations Secretary-General in July 2006 and it was first convened in October/ November 2006. The formation of the IGF was first recommended in the report of the Working Group on Internet Governance following a series of open consultations. This report was one of the inputs to the second phase of the WSIS in Tunis in 2005, which formally called for the creation of the IGF and set out its mandate. Following an open consultation meeting held in February 2006, the UN Secretary-General established an Advisory Group, the MAG, and a Secretariat as the main institutional bodies of the IGF.

The library and information systems also have major responsibilities in creating awareness about changes in information seeking patterns among the information clientele. Drastic changes in information locating trends in the knowledge society have left deep impact particularly on library and information systems. The librarians are no longer document-keepers, but function as information-generators and knowledge-managers in this context of paradigm shift. However, it is not only Information and Communication Technology (ICT) that is driving the changes in library and information systems and services. The other reason is changing trends in our educational systems. The capacity building in information seeking skill is highly relevant to cope up with the ongoing trend of education, where the importance is given not to mere memorizing any fact, but on one's efficiency in locating right bit of information in quickest possible time. There was opinion that the current educational system must change, or society must face the consequences. Some have argued that the education system must change purely because it is a system originally set up to meet the needs of the industrial revolution, and is now therefore outmoded. The industrial revolution demanded the synchronisation of human behaviour with machinery, and mass education was instrumental in preparing generations of regimented workers. Information and Communication Technologies (ICT) have already made a significant impact on higher education to change forever the face of traditional education. The contemporary information society doesn't demand a flock of closely controlled workers with mere mechanized monotonous efficiency, but groups of fresh well-trained professionals with acute skill of finding out the right information with right bit at right instant in right way for the right clientele from the ocean of information. The demand for more knowledge in the information society has resulted in an increase of subjects offered in higher education. A glance through a decade-old prospectus and a comparison of the same with this year's from the same university will undoubtedly show that there has been a big increase in the number of courses offered, and the diversity in range of subject matter. This is a consequence of universities diversifying in an attempt to capture new student populations. Furthermore, the subjects are becoming so specialized, that the academic viability of traditional subjects are continuously squeezing. The traditional subjects are proliferating continuously in several specialized components due to information overload in a particular discipline. The universities must keep pace with this changing environment by delivering courses that are both economically viable and high in quality, or they must diversify using a strategy based on distributed learning. The library and information resource centers should also amend strategies of services to the information seekers.

For instance, a research scholar, whose area of research is, say, Fermi Liquid (a specific subject under condensed matter physics); hardly asks about all papers published on that subject in a particular year. But he'll make query about the thrust areas of research of the subject for a stipulated time-period, or he may ask about extinct areas in a particular subject, or he may ask about stable areas of research over a long time, or he may ask about current trend of research, or latest state-of-the-art etc. These types of queries could be answered only if the information service provider considers not only the macroscopic documents, but also the sustainability and potency of relevant keywords from the published literature to examine it critically, so that the information at microscopic level could be retrieved. The thorough look at the microscopic level only contemplates the current modes of changing information need. In this way they can maintain the quality using technology whilst optimizing the time and resources of well-qualified information professional to support services.

New technological innovations and radical changes in our education system brought another new era prevailed over the information-based society to take a new turn towards the post-modern society since late eighties of the last century, which is utterly knowledge-based. It is knowledge, which is the main driving force of this post-modern, post-information-based society. Knowledge is the power and fuel of any sort of functional engines within the domain of current socio-economic infrastructure. Knowledge accumulates information; and information, in turn broaden the spectrum of knowledge. The outlook towards wealth and poverty in this context has also been somehow molded. The financial poverty is rather preferable to info-poverty and the info-richness is preferable to financial-richness. Information is an omnipresent resource today, but it is a resource only when processed rationally and scientifically; and organized in a logical sequence and used profitably. Unorganized information causes information overload and documentary chaos. Unprocessed information gives rise to information loss, and unorganized information allows retrieval of irrelevant information that causes noise in an information system. Unorganized and unprocessed information just add junk to the multitudes of documents. The processing and organisation of information is thus a crucial function that will be discussed in the next chapter.

3

Information Processing and Knowledge Organization : Traditional Ways

Traditionally, information processing and organization essentially turns into document processing and organization. The basic functions involved in document processing and organization are: classification, cataloguing, indexing & abstracting. "Classification is the sleeping beauty of library and information science," said Hanne Albrechtsen (*http://www.encyclopedia.com/doc/1G1-54050958.html*). The library classification focuses on the classification system as a representational tool used to organize a collection of information resources. Classification as process involves the orderly and systematic assignment of each entity to one and only one class within a system of mutually exclusive and non-overlapping classes. General classification theory is based on four principles (Richmond, 1990):

1) Every thing, object etc. has to have a distinct and unambiguous description of its unique qualities
2) Principles involving likeness and distinctness must be used in creating classes
3) Hierarchies and other relational methods are necessary in order to group fundamental characteristics and to identify fundamental differences clearly
) The final system should appear as a logical progression from general to specific

Classification is exemplified by the discipline of taxonomy. Broadly defined, taxonomy is the science of classification, or, as Mayr (1982) defines it, "the theory and practice of delimiting kinds of organisms". Originally the term taxonomy referred to the classifying of living organisms (now known as alpha taxonomy); however, the term is now applied in a wider, more general sense and now may refer to "Classification" of things, as well as to the "Principles" underlying such a classification. Taxonomy is a high-level, hierarchical classification of information for execution of scientific documentation that facilitates the management of recorded information throughout its life cycle. Its focus is on the purpose of information within and how it is used across the information clientele in the said domain of specified subject. Each subject domain requires a different taxonomy because each has unique content, semantic relationships, target group and histories. A taxonomy indicates classification of items within subject domains. This is highly effective in today's information access difficulties. As it functions within specific subject domains, taxonomy doesn't necessarily use pre-existing classification schemes, but it is often based on a synthesis derived from user need and language. Like traditional library and information science classification arrangements, it can be hierarchical systems that also use controlled vocabularies and thesauri, but it is not always based on the accepted standards used in a traditional library setting. The multifaceted subject headings of taxonomy have the added advantage of reflecting topology involved in a semantic structure, or ontology, allowing for potentially wider consultation and application of knowledge objects. Taxonomies leave room for growth and constant revision, depending on external or internal factors. Taxonomies encompass many different aspects of information; for example, content, metadata and metadata repositories, navigation architectures, search architectures, and portal architectures. Taxonomies can be constructed by building on the many practices typically considered part of the librarian's skill set, such as analysis, abstracting, research skills, cataloguing and classification systems, synthesis, subject headings, controlled vocabularies, indexing and thesauri. The objectives of taxonomic investigation are to provide an orderly and systematic organization of knowledge. It identifies the defining characteristics that distinguish an entity; and, based on those characteristics, place the entity within a hierarchical ordering of mutually exclusive superordinate and subordinate classes in accordance with a set of established and widely accepted principles.

All entities, viz. animate objects, inanimate objects, places, concepts, events, properties, and relationships — may be classified according to some taxonomic scheme. The term taxonomy may also apply to relationship schemes other than genus-species hierarchies, such as network structures with different types of relationships. Taxonomies may include single species with multi-genus, for example, "Stone" may appear under several subjects like "Geology", "Archaeology", "Civil engineering" et al. The geologist will study the intrinsic nature of the stone, the archaeologist will concern about the age and site of residence of the same, while the civil engineer will be interested about strength and concreteness. Similarly the entity "Rose" can appear under the following subjects, viz. "Floriculture", "Painting", "Photography" and "Plant pathology". The corresponding information in context for each subjects are — "Breeding of rose plant", "Colour and appearance of the petals", "Photographic features" and "Disease afflicting the plant" respectively. The entity "Blood" is connected simultaneously to "Haematology", "Criminology" and "Molecular cell biology". As the entities are related to several disciplines, the disciplines are also inter-related. For instance, "Haematology" is linked with "Criminology"; and "Floriculture" has some links with "Plant pathology". A taxonomy is a simple organization of different kinds of things or entities into groups. The entities are represented by keywords. The keywords occur in list of controlled vocabularies like List of Subject Headings or Thesauri. The taxonomy is thus closely related with keywords. Selection of appropriate keyword is a crucial factor in developing a scientific taxonomy in a logical sequence. In current usage within "Knowledge Management", taxonomies are seen as less broad than ontologies as ontologies apply a larger variety of relation types. Mathematically, a hierarchical taxonomy is a tree structure of classifications for a given set of objects. At the top of this structure is a single classification, the root node, which applies to all objects. Nodes below this root are more specific classifications that apply to subsets of the total set of classified objects. So for instance, in common schemes of scientific classification of organisms, the root is called "Organism" followed by nodes for the taxonomic ranks: Domain, kingdom, phylum, class, etc. The progress of reasoning proceeds from the general to the more specific.

In the cataloguing process, librarians create MARC records, in which aspects of a document are analyzed and entered into the record as metadata. These skills are applicable to facet taxonomies. Hierarchical taxonomy directly reflects the broader-term and narrower-term relationships and makes the notion of authority control apparent in traditional subject headings. Further, the process of synthesis can be applied in both instances to more accurately render concepts or contents. This semantic structure is another form of controlled vocabulary or authority control.

The information explosion reality of today's knowledge society throws challenge to the existing LIS skills. The additional competencies and mindsets would be useful, especially with regard to taxonomy development in chaotic information overload situation. Lateral thinking and general contextual awareness are also important abilities when visualizing multifaceted applications of subject headings that reflect as much as possible the relationships and value of knowledge objects to their user groups. Also, the traditional book-library focus must be broadened to include other kinds of libraries, information centers, and users.

Taxonomy can help for continuous updating and dynamic amendment of a system, but the creation of taxonomy needs proper knowledge of classification and other subject access tools. The dynamic nature of the knowledge environment necessitates continuous monitoring, evaluation, and appropriate adjustments to the taxonomy to keep it relevant and valuable. This is very different from traditional classifications, which change slowly or allow synthesis only with many rules and regulations or conferences with peers. The existing library classification schemes should emphasize synthesis and taxonomy development to better prepare library and information professionals for all aspects of the current information environment and that of the future. An understanding of natural language processing, ontology and the potential of keyword searching would help in determining how best to organize information and make it available. Indexing is also an information retrieval tool that is applicable to the world of taxonomy.

A classification scheme mandates that an entity can be a member of one and only one class, it provides for communication of meaningful information through the systematic and principled ordering of classes. Furthermore, it establishes and enforces stability of reference by providing each class with a unique label that links individual members of the class to the class definition. Shera (1950) observed that, throughout history, attempts to classify knowledge have based on four fundamental assumptions:

- Universal order
- Unity of knowledge
- Similarity of class members
- Intrinsic essence
  - The assumption of "Universal order" posits an immutable conception of reality that serves as a unifying framework for all knowledge.
  - The assumption of "Unity of knowledge" presupposes that past, present, and future knowledge can be represented within a single, inclusive hierarchy of superordinate and subordinate classes.
  - The assumption of "Similarity of class members" holds that a class can be defined by a set of essential features and that these features are shared by all members of the class and distinguishes that class from all other classes in the structure, and
  - The assumption of "Intrinsic essence" maintains that there is a set of individually necessary and jointly sufficient features that is intrinsic to all members of a class and that these features constitute the essence of the class.

Traditionally, bibliographic classifications have been

deductive, top-down schemes that enumerate a set of mutually exclusive classes. An enumerative classification scheme begins with a universe of knowledge and a theory of organization or set of principles that establishes the conceptual structure of the scheme. Whether the universe encompasses all knowledge or is limited to a specific domain, construction of the scheme involves the logical process of division and subdivision of the original universe such that each class, or each level of classes in the structure, is differentiated by a particular characteristic or property (e.g., the property "colour" or "shape"). The result is a hierarchical structure of generic (genus/species) relationships wherein each subordinate class is, theoretically, a true species of the superordinate within which it is nested.

Faceted (analytico-synthetic) classification systems are inductive, bottom-up schemes generated through a process of analysis and synthesis. Construction of the faceted structure begins with the analysis of universe of knowledge to identify the individual elements, properties and features, of the universe. These elements are then organized into mutually exclusive groups on the basis of conceptual similarity, and these groups are, in turn, arranged in successively larger groupings to form facets that can be used to represent entities in the universe. In this way, meaningful relationships are established not only between the elements in a group but between the groups themselves. The result is a controlled vocabulary of concepts and their associated labels that can he used, in association with a notation and a prescribed citation order, to synthesize the classes that will populate the classification scheme. A faceted vocabulary for classifying "Stone" may include mutually exclusive facets for "Colour" (red, grey, black); "State" (crystalline, amorphous), and "shape" (spherical, tetrahedron, dodecahedron). Following the citation order shape—state—color, classes would be constructed by selecting a single value, or isolate, from each facet. Examples of the classes that could be constructed in this faceted scheme would be tetrahedron—crystalline—grey and spherical—amorphous—black.

As a faceted classification scheme adheres to a fixed citation order during the construction of individual classes, the resulting structure, like an enumerative scheme, is necessarily hierarchical. In fact, it is the hierarchical nature of bibliographic classification schemes that allows for the arrangement of physical resources on the shelves of the library. "Reading" a classification scheme involves moving down the hierarchy, from superordinate to subordinate and from left to right, to generate a series of relationships between classes that can be translated into the linear order of the library shelf. It is just this linear structure that Ranganathan captured in the notion of APUPA (or Alien-Penumbral-Umbral-Penumbral-Alien). The umbral class (U) represents the focal topic; penumbral classes (P) are those most closely related to the focal topic; and alien classes (A) are those removed from and therefore unrelated to the focal topic. When the individual reviews a collection of resources arranged in classified order, he generally begins with the most relevant class or focal topic (U); moving either to the right or the left, he progresses from resources on the focal topic through closely related materials (P) to those resources which are unrelated (A). In this fashion, the linearity inherent in the hierarchical structure of a classification scheme is used to create a meaningful context by bringing into proximity those classes within the hierarchical structure which are theoretically most closely related. In other words, a bibliographic classification establishes a controlled vocabulary in the form of a set of uniquely labeled classes that serve both to define and to organize the intellectual content of a collection of resources. Furthermore, this vocabulary determines the conceptual boundaries of the scheme's universe by including only the knowledge that is relevant within the immediate universe. The resulting arrangement is meaningful precisely because it constitutes a principled context for information, which is a context shaped by class definitions, by information-bearing, hierarchical relationships and by meaningful distinctions between classes and, by extension, between the concepts that those classes represent.

The existing library classification schemes thus define subject content through schedules of classes, divisions and sections that shift from general to specific. A successful classification scheme is one that saves the time of the user by creating an ordered document profile that perfectly matches the user's profile. Like a library, the Internet is a store of information packages, but without systematic order. Lynch (1997) claims that the Internet is merely a huge amount of disorganized data, a "chaotic repository for the collective output of the world's digital printing presses". Search engines furnish access and retrieval points for Internet resources but not all of them allow users to navigate using subject categories. Classification of web resources is an active topic of research today. Existing schemes assign alphanumeric notation to each and every keyword for an ordered shelf-arrangement, whereas, in case of web resources no such notation is needed. The crucial factor for web resource management is to derive relationships among different keywords. Several groups of keywords in a subject area indicate corresponding specific areas under that subject. Such keyword groups consist of numbers of inter-related keywords or keyword-clusters. The keyword-cluster-analysis is prime function for organization of web resources. The fundamental step towards keyword-cluster-analysis involves categorization of keywords, which are discussed in the forthcoming chapters. Before switching over to keywords, let us discuss information categories and some key aspects of the present information age, viz. information explosion, overloading and control in the next few chapters. The comprehensive list of general classification schemes and different cataloguing codes are furnished in Table 1 and Table 2 respectively. These are generally regarded as most effective tool for organizing knowledge efficiently in traditional ways.

Table 3.1 : General classification schemes

Sl. No.	*Name of classification scheme*	*Year*	*Founder*	*Place*	*Type of classification scheme*
1	Dewey Decimal Classification	1876	Melville Louis Kossuth Dewey	USA	Almost Enumerative Scheme
2	Expansive Classification (EC)	1882	Charles Ammi Cutter	Boston (USA)	Almost Enumerative
3	Library of Congress Classification (LCC)	1897	Library of Congress (Hertbert Putnam)	USA	Fully Enumerative Scheme of Classification
4	Subject Classification	1897	James Duff Brown	London (UK)	Fully Enumerative
5	Universal Decimal Classification (UDC)	1905	Henry La Fontaine & Paul Otlet	Brussels (Belgium)	Almost Faceted Scheme
6	Colon Classification (CC)	1933	Siyali Ramamrita Ranganathan	Bangalore (India)	1st to 3rd Ed. Is Rigidly Faceted Scheme and 4th to 7th ed. Freely Faceted Scheme
7	Bibliographic Classification (BC)	1940	Henry Evelyn Bliss [2nd edtion developed in Britain since 1977]	New York (USA)	Almost Faceted Scheme
8	International Classification Scheme	1961	Fremout Rider	USA	Fully Enumerative
9	Broad System of Ordering (3rd ed) (BSO)	1978	FID	USA	Faceted

Table 3.2: Different codes of cataloguing

Sl. No.	*Year*	*Name of code*	*Founder*
1	1841	British Museum Code (BMC)	Anthony Panizzi
2	1852	Jewett Code	Charles C. Jewett
3	1876	Rules for Dictionary Catalogue (RDC)	Charles Ammi Cutter
4	1899	Prussian Instructions (PI)	K A Linderfelt
5	1899	The German cataloguing code	K. Dziatzko
6	1908	Anglo American Code/Joint Code (AAC)	American Library Association, Library Association
7	1927	Vatican Code (VC)	Vatican Library, J.C.M. Hanson, W.W. Bishop
8	1934	Classified Catalogue Code (CCC)	Siyali Ramamrita Ranganathan
9	1949	American Library Association Code (ALAC)/1st ed. 1941	American Library Association
10	1960	Code of Cataloging Rules (CCR)	Seymour Lubetzky
11	1967	Anglo American Cataloguing Rules – I (AACR – I) (Consisted of two texts, North American Text and British Text that varied widely)	American Library Association, Library of Congress, Library Association, Canadian Library Association
12	1977	Nippon Cataloguing Rules (NCR)	The Committee of Cataloguing, Japan Library Association
13	1978	Anglo American Cataloguing Rules – II(AACR – II)	American Library Association, Canadian Library Association, Library Association Publishing, Chartered Institute of Library and Information Professionals
14	1988	Anglo American Cataloguing Rules – II R (AACR – II R)	—Do—
15	1998	FRBR (Functional Requirements for Bibliographic Records)	International Federation of Library Associations (IFLA)
16	2010	RDA (Resources Description and Access)	American Library Association, Canadian Library Association, Chartered Institute of Library and Information Professionals

4

Information Processing and Knowledge Organization : New Orientations

Knowledge Organization (KO) is one of the crucial contemporary fields, which plays major role in communicating and exchanging knowledge. The field KO is closely linked with LIS and addresses different learning and research activities. In the context of LIS, Knowledge Organization (KO) indicates activities such as document description, indexing and classification performed in libraries, bibliographical databases, archives etc. by librarians, archivists, information specialists, subject specialists et al. As a subject domain, KO is concerned with the nature and quality of different ways of knowledge organizing processes (KOP) as well as the knowledge organizing systems (KOS) used to organize documents, document representations, works and concepts. Library and Information Science (LIS) may be regarded as the central discipline of KO. Hjorland opined this implication of KO as the narrow meaning.

According to him, the broader meaning is KO also exists that deals about the social division of mental labor, i.e. the organization of universities and other institutions for research and higher education, the structure of disciplines and professions, the social organization of media, the production and dissemination of "knowledge" etc. We may distinguish between the social organization of knowledge on one hand, and on the other hand the intellectual or cognitive organization of knowledge. The broad sense is thus both about how knowledge is socially organized and how reality is organized. The uncovering of structures of reality is done by the single sciences, e.g. chemistry, biology, geography and linguistics. Well known examples are the periodic system in chemistry and biological taxonomy. Generalized theories about the structure of reality, such as *the theory of integrative levels* first enunciated by Auguste Comte belong to the philosophical disciplines "metaphysics" and "ontology".

Different approaches of KO were suggested by Broughton; Hansson; Hjørland & López-Huertas (2005) as follows:

1. The traditional approach to KO expressed by classification systems used in libraries and databases, including DDC, LCC and UDC
2. The facet-analytical approach founded by Ranganathan about 1933 and further developed by the British Classification Research Group
3. The information retrieval tradition (IR) founded in the 1950s.
4. User oriented / cognitive views gaining influence from the 1970s
5. Bibliometric approaches following Garfield's construction of the *Science Citation Index* in 1963
6. The domain analytic approach (first formulated about 1994)

7. Other approaches (Among recent suggestions are semiotic approaches, "critical-hermeneutical" approaches discourse-analytic approaches and genre-based approaches. An important trend is also an emphasis on document representations, document typology and description, mark up languages, document architectures etc.)

Each of the six approaches is discussed below.

1. The traditional approach : The two distinguished personalities, viz. Melvil Dewey (1851-1931) and Henry Bliss (1870-1955) may be reckoned as Father Figure in traditional library classification, or broadly speaking, knowledge organization. Eugene Garfield wrote about Bliss: "His goals and aspirations were different from those of Melvil Dewey, whom he certainly surpassed in intellectual ability, but by whom he was dwarfed in organizational ability and drive. Dewey was a businessman, but he was in no sense as profound in his accomplishments." (Garfield 1975, 252). This difference in the character of the two men is reflected in their approach to knowledge organization as also reflected by Miksa's (1998, pp. 42-45) presentation of the business perspective of Melvil Dewey. Dewey's business approach is hardly an intellectual approach on which the field can find a theoretical foundation for KO understood as an academic discipline. His interest was not to find an optimal system to support users of libraries, but rather to find an efficient way to manage library collections. He was interested in developing a system which could be used in many libraries, a standardized way to manage library collections.

According to Broughton et al, "DDC should thus be seen as the dream of the library administrator rather than the dream of the library user. It is not designed for any specific collection and must be seen as a compromise between different collections and corresponding scholarly interests. In order to minimize the work load in libraries, the system is conservative in the sense that it often prefers to avoid to change structure. In other words: Internal consistency over different editions has often taken priority compared to updating the system in order to make it more in accordance with the surrounding society. The user does not get a detailed, realistic view about relations between disciplines and fields of knowledge, but the library administrator gets a system in which most of the books are already classified by other libraries or agencies and which is used for both shelf arrangement and catalog searching. The library administrator may hire people from library schools, who know the system and may apply this knowledge in all the libraries using DDC. The system is thus also supporting professional interests. It probably represents a rationalization of library work more than anything else. Its main quality may be that it represents a standard not a system optimized for browsing or retrieval for any particular interest. It should be added that what is today called *Library and Information Science*, LIS, was termed *library economy* in 1876 when the system was first published, which is also an indication of the administrative rather than the academic goals of the system. This may also explain why systems designed on the basis of more modern principles have not succeeded in influencing practice in libraries. Among the other principles, which may be attributed to the traditional approach to KO are:

- Principle of controlled vocabulary
- Cutter's rule about specificity
- Hulme's principle of literary warrant (1911)
- Principle of organizing from the general to the specific

The principle of controlled vocabulary is essentially a way of avoiding synonyms and homonyms as indexing terms by using standardized vocabulary. Cutter's rule states that it is always the most specific, most appropriate expressions that should be looked up in the vocabulary of notations and assigned to documents. In this way the expressions for the topics to be made retrievable are rendered most predictable. The term "literary warrant" as well as the basic principle underlying this expression was introduced by E. Wyndham Hulme (1911, p. 447). Hulme discusses whether, for example, the periodic system of chemistry should be used for book classification. He writes (p. 46-47):

> "In Inorganic Chemistry what has philosophy to offer? [Philosophy here meaning science, which produced the periodic system]. It is merely a classification by the names of the elements for which practically no literature in book form exists. No monograph, for instance, has yet been published on the Chemistry of Iron or Gold.
>
> . . .
>
> Hence we must turn to our second alternative which bases definition upon a purely literary warrant. According to this principle definition is merely the result of an accurate survey and measurement of classes in literature. A class heading is warranted only when a literature in book form has been shown to exist, and the test of the validity of a heading is the degree of accuracy with which it describes the area of subject matter common to the class. Definition [of classes or subject headings], therefore, may be described as the plotting of areas pre-existing in literature. To this literary warrant a quantitative value can be assigned so soon as the bibliography of a subject has been definitely compiled. The real classifier of literature is the book-wright, the so-called book classifier is merely the recorder. Hulme (1911, p. 46-47).

The principle of ordering from general subjects to specific subjects is generally acknowledged and may be related to an essentialist way of understanding.

Today, after more than 100 years of research and development in LIS, the "traditional" approach still has a strong position in KO and in many ways its principles still dominate.

The traditional approach, however, shows signs of certain vagueness in its theoretical and methodological basis. Is it subject knowledge rather than competency in KO that marks the construction and administration of knowledge organizing systems? Often it seems to be assumed that that the organization of knowledge is just a matter of "reading" the *correct relations between concepts*. There is not much indication of how this is done. Although debates about the philosophy of science, e.g. in relation to positivism, was not unknown among the founding fathers of knowledge organization, they were not particularly clear on this point and the same is also the case with the ordinary practice of KO. It is with the development of the domain-analytic approach that the question about the subjectivity and objectivity of KO in a systematic way is first built into the methodological foundation of KO".

2. The facet-analytical approach (Broughton et al, 2005) : The publication of S. R. Ranganathan's *Colon Classification* in 1933 started a new era of this approach that was further developed by the British Classification Research Group. This approach is based on analytico-synthetic methodology. The term "analysis" means, breaking down each subject into its basic concepts. While the term synthesis means, combining the relevant units and concepts to describe the subject matter completely.

The subjects are first analyzed into some fundamental categories as proposed by Ranganathan: Personality, Matter, Energy, Space and Time:

- Personality is the distinguishing characteristic of a subject
- Matter is the physical material of which a subject may be composed
- Energy is any action that occurs with respect to the subject
- Space is the geographic component of the location of a subject.
- Time is the period associated with a subject.

S. R. Ranganathan wrote in his 'Philosophy of Library Classification' (1951):

> "An enumerative scheme with a superficial foundation can be suitable and even economical for a closed system of knowledge. . . . What distinguishes the universe of current knowledge is that it is a dynamical continuum. It is ever growing; new branches may stem from any of its infinity of points at any time; they are unknowable at present. They can not therefore be enumerated here and now; nor can they be anticipated, their filiations can be determined only after they appear." (Ranganathan 1951).

Ranganathan expressed the views:

1. That enumerative systems have a superficial foundation
2. That the discovery of new knowledge cannot be anticipated in an enumerative system
3. That the discovery of new knowledge can be anticipated in a faceted system (based on the view that new knowledge is formed by combination of a priori existing categories)

La Barre (2006) found that faceted techniques are increasingly being used in the design of web-pages. A specific format, XFML, a simple XML format for exchanging metadata in the form of faceted hierarchies has been developed (Van Dijck 2003). The technique is thus very alive and in use.

3. The information retrieval approach (IR) (Broughton et al, 2005) : Information retrieval (IR) and knowledge organization (KO) are normally considered two different but closely related subfields within Library and Information Science (LIS) - related to respectively search labor and description labor (cf., Warner 2002). They are, however, trying to solve the same kind of problems: enabling users to find relevant information.

The important landmark in the IR-appraoch is the Cranfield experiments, which were founded in the 1950s, and the TREC experiments (Text Retrieval Conferences) starting in 1992. It was the Cranfield experiments, which introduced the famous measures "recall" and "precision" as evaluation criteria for systems efficiency. The Cranfield experiments found that classification systems like UDC and facet-analytic systems were less efficient compared to free-text searches or low level indexing systems ("UNITERM"). The Cranfield I test found according to Ellis (1996, 3-6) the following results.

UNITERM	82,0% recall
Alphabetical subject headings	81,5% recall
UDC	75,6% recall
Facet classification scheme	73,8% recall

Although these results have been criticized and questioned, the IR-tradition became much more influential while library classification research lost influence.

4. User-oriented approach (Broughton et al, 2005): This approach encounters following issues:

- User-friendly knowledge organization
- Market-oriented knowledge organization
- Knowledge organization based on empirical studies of users

- Knowledge organization done by users (e.g. the recent trend in folksonomies).

The best way to define this approach is probably by systems based upon user-oriented approaches that must specify how the design of a system is made on the basis of empirical studies of users. Hjørland (2007a) found that user oriented view seem to have driven out the study of documents and that they have made some problematic critiques of "the bibliographical paradigm". User-oriented views are often contrasted with "the systems driven approach" which is again associated with the Cranfield experiments.

5. Bibliometric approaches (Broughton et al, 2005) : These approaches are primarily based on using bibliographical references to organize networks of papers, mainly by bibliographic coupling (introduced by Kessler 1963) or co-citation analysis (independently suggested by Marshakova 1973 and Small 1973). In recent years it has become a popular activity to construe bibliometric maps as structures of research fields.

The following issues are important in considering bibliometric approaches to KO:

- The level of indexing depth is partly determined by the number of terms assigned to each document. In citation indexing this corresponds to the number of references in a given paper. On the average, scientific papers contain 10-15 references, which provide quite a high level of depth.
- The references, which function as access points, are provided by the highest subject-expertise: The experts writing in the leading journals. This expertise is much higher than that which library catalogs or bibliographical databases typically are able to draw on.

6. The domain analytic approach (DA) (Broughton et al, 2005) : The domain analytic approach is an approach formulated at the beginning of the 1990s as an alternative to the dominant cognitive view in LIS. It is a sociological-epistemological standpoint. The indexing of a given document should reflect the needs of a given group of users or a given ideal purpose. In other words, any description or representation of a given document is more or less suited to the fulfillment of certain tasks. A description is never objective or neutral, and the goal is not to standardize descriptions or make one description once and for all for different target groups. It is the only approach to KO which has seriously examined epistemological issues in the field, i.e. comparing the assumptions made in different approaches to KO and examining the questions regarding subjectivity and objectivity in KO. Subjectivity is not just about individual differences. Such differences are of minor interest because they cannot be used as guidelines for KO. What seems important are collective views shared by many users. A kind of subjectivity about many users is related to philosophical positions. In any field of knowledge different views are always at play. In arts, for example, different views of art are always present. Such views determine views on art works, writing on art works, how art works are organized in exhibitions and how writings on art are organized in libraries (Ørom 2003). In general it can be stated that different philosophical positions on any issue have implications for relevance criteria, information needs and for criteria of organizing knowledge.

....

Cutter, Bliss, and other important classification researchers from the period of the second half of the 19th century and the first half of the 20st century, realized, that what is organized cannot be taken as absolute truth. However, Bliss believed that knowledge was relatively safe and true, which is why a kind of consensus could be established. Because of this, Bliss and his contemporary chose the term "knowledge organization", "knowledge" understood in the Platonic tradition as "verified, true belief".

In his preface to Bliss (1929), the philosopher John Dewey wrote:

> "A classification of books to be effective on the practical side must correspond to the relationships of subject-matters, and this correspondence can be secured only as the intellectual, or conceptual, organization is based upon the order inherent in the fields of knowledge, which in turn mirrors the order of nature." (Dewey 1929, p. viii)

This quote is in accordance with the traditional view of knowledge as a neutral and objective reflection of reality. It is, however, a bad representation of John Dewey's pragmatic view of knowledge and of classification, as demonstrated by another quote:

> "No sensible person tries to do everything. He has certain main interests and leading aims by which he makes his behaviour coherent and effective. To have an aim is to limit, select, concentrate, group. Thus a basis is furnished for selecting and organizing things according as their ways of acting are related to carrying forward pursuit. Cherry trees will be differently grouped by woodworkers, orchardists, artists, scientists and merry-makers. To the execution of different purposes different ways of acting and re-acting on the part of trees are important. Each classification may be equally sound when the difference of ends is borne in mind.

Nevertheless there is a genuine objective standard for the goodness of special classifications. One will further the cabinetmaker in reaching his end while another will hamper him. One classification will assist the botanist in carrying on fruitfully his work of inquiry, and another will retard and confuse him. The teleological theory of classification does not therefore commit us to the notion that classes are purely verbal or purely mental. Organization is no more merely nominal or mental in any art, including the art of inquiry, than it is in a department store or railway system. The necessity of execution supplies objective criteria. Things have to be sorted out and arranged so that their grouping will promote successful action for ends. Convenience, economy and efficiency are the bases of classification, but these things are not restricted to verbal communication with others nor to inner consciousness; they concern objective action. They must take effect in the world.

At the same time, a classification is not a bare transcript or duplicate of some finished and done-for arrangement pre-existing in nature. It is rather a repertory of weapons for attack upon the future and the unknown. For success, the details of past knowledge must be reduced from bare facts to meanings, the fewer, simpler and more extensive the better... " (Dewey 1920/1948, p. 151-154).

This quote clearly demonstrates that John Dewey did not accept the mirror metaphor of knowledge, or, as he expressed it: "a bare transcript or duplicate of some finished and done-for arrangement pre-existing in nature".

Two different views of knowledge can be contrasted in the context of KO:

- "Positivist view": Knowledge and KO as "a bare transcript or duplicate of some finished and done-for arrangement pre-existing in nature".
- "Pragmatic view": Knowledge and KO as something constructed to deal with some human needs and interests.

The pragmatist view of knowledge is also connected with "fallibilism", the view that scientific research is never to be taken finally proved, that new evidence may change scientific beliefs. The implication of fallibilism is that we cannot understand the documents as representing knowledge, as traditionally understood. We should not talk about knowledge or knowledge organization, but about knowledge claims and the organization of knowledge claims. The implication is that each knowledge claim is supported by and connected with arguments, theories and world views. If this is recognized by the people performing KO, then the activity is not based on "positivism".

5

Different Categories of Information

Information may be categorized into following classes on the basis of different parameters. The categorization against some parameters is listed below:

Depending on organization of contents

- Structured information (Information having unambiguous meaning and explicitly presentable within the format of the data. The example of structured information is a relational database table)
- Unstructured information (The meaning is droopily implied by its form and therefore need clarification in order to extract the actual sense. The examples are natural language documents, still images, audio-visual materials etc.)

Depending on creation of contents

- Fundamental information (Obtained from primary sources of information)
- Repackaged information (Obtained from secondary and tertiary sources of information)

Depending on nature of contents

- Factual information (Database, statement of a thing executed or existing etc.)
- Analytic information (Critical appraisal, view, judgment, commentaries etc.)
- Objective information (It is integrated information on all sides of a topic like web site, handbook, encyclopedia etc.)
- Subjective information (It is evaluative information on some specific side(s) of a topic like review article or editorial page of newspaper)

Depending on life-cycle of contents

- Active (frequently used)
- Less Active (less frequently used)
- Historical (very less frequently used)
- Archived (rarely used)

Depending on nature of containers of information or information sources

- Primary (Scholarly journal articles Theses, dissertations, government reports, symposia and conference proceedings, original artwork, poems, photographs, speeches, telephonic messages, letters, personal narratives, diaries, interviews, autobiographies, webblogs, e-mail correspondence etc.)
- Secondary (Dictionaries, encyclopedias, textbooks, edited works, biographies, literary criticism and interpretation, political analyses and commentaries, directories, guide books, manuals, handbooks, yearbook, almanac, websites etc.)
- Tertiary (Fact books, Wikipedia, bibliographies (may also be secondary), bibliography of bibliographies, indexing and abstracting sources etc.)

Depending on the physical form of containers of information

- Printed information (All printed materials)
- Non-printed information (other than electronic media) [Magnetic tape, microfiche, microfilm, filmstrip, magnetic drum)
- Electronic information (CD-ROM, DVD-ROM, hard disc etc.)
- Online information (e-mail, voice-mail, SMS)
- Web information (web sites, web blogs, wiki, search engines, you tube etc.)

Depending on levels of perception by information clientele

- Popular information (Information on any subject or topic at popular level for mass)
- State-of-the-art information (Information on any topic revealing different stages of amendment and trends at different time periods)
- Scholarly information (Information on a subject at high academic and research level)

Depending on sphere of interaction of information clientele

- Personal information (Information needed by individuals in their personal life within the circles of family, friends and other close associates)
- Professional information (Information needed by individuals and also groups to maintain and develop their professional career)
- Community information (Information needed by groups for maintaining regular life rhythm of their respective social or cultural community)

Depending on area of interest of information clientele

- Science information
- Social science information
- Cognitive information etc.

Depending on physical and mental need of information clientele

- Psychological information
- Health information etc.

All people are living in envelop of information. The information field is constantly wrapping our thoughts. Our life starts daily with a handful of information on newspaper. Here some broad and major categories of information have been chalked out. Besides, there are so many categories depending on so many parameters and transmitted through so many channels. Information is received by the human brain in the forms of some statements through text, graphics, data, image, sound and many more. The intrinsic truths of nature and human conscience are unveiled by the bits of information. Information is the carrier of truth. The physicist Neils Bohr (1885-1962) said, "The opposite of a correct statement is a false statement. The opposite of a profound truth may well be another profound truth." The truth is unique and evergreen. If it is misinterpreted anyhow, then that's due to the imperfection and limitation of either information creator, or information source and/or information channel. Such misinterpretation may occur due to chaotic flow of unorganized information. The notable point is thus all categories of information are useful only when organized in a logical sequence. Unorganized information brings complete chaos, and is useless. The numbers of information transmitting channels are also growing very fast. Practically, channels are growing faster than the growth rate of information. A bit of information is transmitting so many times through so many channels, and thus replicated. Replication of information is one of the major causes of information overloading. We, the recipients of information should develop our own filter to scan unwanted and irrelevant information. We should control information, before information make a control over us. Information overload and control are very crucial problems in the present age, to be discussed in next chapters.

6

Information Explosion & Information Overloading

This is the age of information explosion. It is a cliché today that we are all drowning in too much information. It is very difficult to navigate on this information ocean, if we do not have an effective information control strategy. Information explosion is an all-pervaded phenomenon today and, also it is the direct consequence of the incessant expansion of the Universe of Knowledge, that results proliferation of subjects with non-stop uprise of multi-disciplinarity and inter-disciplinarity of subjects. In his 1963 book "Little Science, Big Science" (released in an expanded edition in 1986 under the title Little Science, Big Science... and Beyond), Derek John De Solla Price discussed the effect of Second World War on scientific growth. He noted that, "the exponential increase after the war is identical with that before . . . . Science is just where it would have been, statistically speaking, and is growing at the same rate as if there had been no war." Many people have tried to quantify the size of the problem and statistics around, often with no firm basis but, nevertheless, scary. Information is life blood of every processional today, especially in the areas of science and technology. Without latest information we will become obsolete in no time. Technology is continuously changing at a drastic pace and information is expanding rapidly, while the need for its consumption is increasing consequently.

Let us read the following statements, taken from various websites and articles:

"As much new information will be available in the next decade as has been discovered in the whole of human history"

"It is estimated that it would take ... seven centuries to read a year's chemical literature"

"There are 550 billion web-connected documents"

"Fifty thousand new book titles appear annually, with 1.5 million books now in print from 20,000 different publishers"

"People could read 24 hours per day, 365 days per year, and never catch up with what is written"

The web site **www.sims.berkeley.edu/research/projects/how-much-info-2003/** contains an article titled "How Much Information?" from which comes the following:

> "... almost 800 MB of [new] recorded information is produced per person each year. It would take about 30 feet of books to store the equivalent of 800 MB of information on paper". An interesting chart stating quantitative measurement of information is also given there, which is presented below:

Title: How Big is an Exabyte?

Kilobyte (KB)

1,000 bytes OR 10^3bytes

2 Kilobytes: A Typewritten page.

100 Kilobytes: A low-resolution photograph.

Megabyte (MB)

1,000,000 bytes OR 10^6 bytes

1 Megabyte: A small novel OR a 3.5 inch floppy disk.

2 Megabytes: A high-resolution photograph.

5 Megabytes: The complete works of Shakespeare.

10 Megabytes: A minute of high-fidelity sound.

100 Megabytes: 1 meter of shelved books.

500 Megabytes: A CD-ROM.

Gigabyte (GB)

1,000,000,000 bytes OR 10^9 bytes

1 Gigabyte: a pickup truck filled with books.

20 Gigabytes: A good collection of the works of Beethoven.

100 Gigabytes: A library floor of academic journals.

Terabyte (TB)

1,000,000,000,000 bytes OR 10^{12} bytes

1 Terabyte: 50000 trees made into paper and printed.

2 Terabytes: An academic research library.

10 Terabytes: The print collections of the U.S. Library of Congress.

400 Terabytes: National Climatic Data Center database.

Petabyte (PB)

1,000,000,000,000,000 bytes OR 10^{15} bytes

1 Petabyte: 3 years of EOS data (2001).

2 Petabytes: All U.S. academic research libraries.

20 Petabytes: Production of hard-disk drives in 1995.

200 Petabytes: All printed material.

Exabyte (EB)

1,000,000,000,000,000,000 bytes OR 10^{18} bytes

2 Exabytes: Total volume of information generated in 1999.

5 Exabytes: All words ever spoken by human beings.

***Source :* www.sims.berkeley.edu/research/projects/how-much-info-2003/**

Drowning in Information!!!
(http://www.claimseducationmagazine.com/pdfs/fall07_f_orderout.pdf)

The phenomenon, "Information explosion" is an effect of industrial revolution, and the advent of "Industrial revolution" was signaled with the invention of printing. The first milestone of information explosion was probably laid down when the broad discipline of natural science split up in physics, chemistry and biology in nineteenth century. Derek J. de Solla Price measured the exponential growth, doubling every 15 years, of science and technology by counting the annual production of science papers. Papers create information, and information, in turn, creates paper. The prime objective of research paper is thus to accelerate more papers in the scientific community. Price also noted that aim of the primary journal, which was developed in 1665 and abstract journals that were introduced around 1830, was to enable researchers to keep up with the findings of other research workers.

Conyers Herring remarked in 1968 that the information explosion sparks a need for creative synthesis of facts and ideas (Herring, C). For efficient access to good science literature new schemes for compression of subject headings should be devised. The researchers are increasingly dependent on review materials to evaluate prior research and thereby plan their own work. Much research work was compromised by an overload of information that is more widely scattered than ever. Half the articles he sampled on solid-state physics reported research that he found to be "trivial," "outdated," duplicative, or "wrong" five years after publication. As time passes nearly all regress in value. The papers of negative value become less harmful as positive papers become outdated (Herring, C).

The essential dismay emerging out of this phenomenon of information explosion includes the shielding of necessary information from the information seekers. Information shielding tends to information loss and information pollution at the same time. Information explosion causes growth of irrelevant information which in turn creates loss of relevant information due to information overload. Information by definition has an axiomatic status to the fact that it's somehow useful or relevant to all. If it's not, it's not information anymore, just a pile of data. Actually, Data + Added value = Information. If we get overloaded, that is actually a lack of information, caused by overload of data. This is one side, where information overload is viewed from the chaos of data. There is other side. Both information overload and information control can also be viewed from psychological aspect. The amount of information manageable to one may be unmanageable to other or same amount of information may be overload to one, while at the same time underload to other. Receiving information or getting informed indicates a state of mind. Therefore, without a thorough understanding of psychology, it's hard to determine the varying levels of distractibility among the information recipients.

Too much information brings mental exhaustion and creates information fatigueness over the brain and mind. Such fatigueness affects our imagination and reduces creativity. The important point is that information overload is a human problem that needs a human solution. Immeasurable bits of information is signaling at every moment, but the analysis of abilities and inabilities of the information professional and clientele are important to manage information and to organize our daily routine. The library and information professionals have to take the initiatives. The library professionals should teach the students and research scholars how to manage information on the web, and how to select most appropriate keyword to start a searching. The librarians should couple the new modes of information management with the traditional document management schemes. The hybrid library systems will be developed in this way. Technology is just a tool for productivity, but not an alternative to human component. It can't exhibit the good judgment of a human being. Technological solutions can only be as good as the people using and developing it. Technology alone won't solve information overload problems, it can only ease them. A true solution to information overloading is based on following three factors:

1. Individual productivity and efficiency (behavioral)
2. Corporate culture and environment (behavioral)
3. Software applications (technology)

When we start to rely solely on the technology to manage information we receive, we slowly lose our own mental abilities. We have to decide how to use information, and when to use information, in order to keep our mental power on. It's a sort of mental atrophy similar to physical atrophy. If we don't exercise our muscles they gradually loose ability to work over time. Similarly if we don't have any regular thought-provoking mental exercise, our brain would be attacked by mental retardedness eventually. The abilities to organize, prioritize and focus the technology thus become a mental crutch. The result of too much dependence on technology is: we'll stop running the technology, but the technology starts running us. Technology can help us to accomplish recurring tasks. But technology can't solve information overload problem alone. The teenagers are now addicted to internet and SMS. It seems that they are plugged into cyber world at all times simply because it's there. It is immaterial whether they truly need it or not. Sometimes we need to step back and ask, "Am I really need to read all these newsfeeds I've subscribed to?"; "Am I roaming through these sites because they really do help me to become more productive?" The library and information professionals have to possess the basic skills to manage information. They should guide the information consumers how to walk on the ways of the cyber world. If any lacking exists there, then technology might become a hindrance rather than a help. It would become a liability and will be a part of the problem. The British physicist Bill Hirst said, "I heard someone tried the monkeys-on-typewriters bit trying for the plays of W. Shakespeare, but all they got was the collected works of Francis Bacon." This is the actual result to be confronted in case of an aimless roaming on cyber space.

It's highly dangerous to be plugged with internet in 24/7. To improve our productivity and ability to manage large amounts of information, sometimes we need mental silence with our cell phone off and laptop offline. Everyone needs to take a step back and look at what the real problem is. If we spend a little more time improving our own abilities to organize our tasks and digest incoming information we'll actually improve the manner in which we use the technology. Unplugged with internet doesn't mean ignorance about information.

According to Mr. Daya Prakash, Head-IT, LG Electronics India, information overload is directly related to the management of IT in a cost and operation efficient manner. He said, "I was going through an article of Bill Gates where he refers to challenges of information overload as well as information under load. According to him staying focused is one issue; that is the problem with information overload. The other problem is information under load. Being flooded with information does not mean we have the right information or that we are in touch with the right people." Vijay Sethi, VP, Information Systems and CIO, Hero Honda Motors, believed that information overload is not a onetime activity but a daily occurrence. It is not easy to track it all, and when one wants to find some information, there are times when one gets lost in a maze, leading to loss of productivity, as one tends to find more information or sift through it. Huge overload of information also leads to stress resulting in a decreased attention span. According to Mr. Arun Gupta, Customer Care Associate and Group CTO, Shopper's Stop, information overload is becoming a problem in some aspects of managing business with organizations demanding information across multiple dimensions for analysis in the form of reports and tactical data from transactional systems.

One of the direct consequences of information overload is "Personal Unproductivity". Our train of thought and workflow are interrupted so many times in a day just for checking e-mail, Googling something insignificant or answering voicemail. Sometimes we are not even aware that we are doing it. It just naturally happened because it is there. According to the management scientist Dr. Donald Wetmore, the average person is interrupted once every eight minutes. Eighty percent of these interruptions are rated as having little-to-no value, creating approximately three hours of wasted time per day. The important point is that we need not scan every piece of information that comes to us through various channels.

Sometimes, we can't pay attention to a single job, but try to concentrate on multiple tasks simultaneously. Multitasking at any instant brings tension and pollutes our brain. In fact, multitasking, outside the context of computers, isn't possible. The effect of multitasking is "Pseudo-Attention Deficit Disorder" (PADD). Too much information creates some sort of phobia in our mind, i.e. phobia of time-deficit. This phobia imparts a mandate to our mind so that we start thinking to scan all information within a short time. We'll get very short time, and we have to finish all jobs in no time with terrific rush – such fearful thought brings some pseudo-deadlines in our mind. These deadlines bring tension that hazes our brain with trepidation, resulting eventually a sort of disorder, known as "Pseudo-Attention Deficit Disorder". Scanning of each and every bit of information is absurd. We have to decide the scope of our task on the basis of our capacity and time available.

One has Pseudo-attention deficit disorder if:

- He/she finds his/her mind wandering from tasks that are uninteresting or difficult
- He/she says things without thinking and later regrets having said them.
- He/she makes quick decisions without thinking enough about their possible bad results
- He/she have a quick temper and a short fuse

- He/she has trouble planning in what order to do a series of tasks or activities
- In group activities it is hard for him/her to wait his/her turn
- He/she usually works on more than one project at a time, and fails to finish many of them

Concentrating on multi-task at the same instant is humanly impossible. According to the psychiatrist Dr. Edward Hallowell, "No one really multitasks. Your brain literally can't multitask. You just spend less time on any one thing. You can't pay attention to two things simultaneously. You're switching back and forth between the two. So you're paying less concerted attention to either one."

The ways of working should be changed to manage all the information coming from every direction. Some major causes of information overload are listed below:

- Obsessive need to be constant surfing or email-checking
- Absentmindedness and lack of attention
- Staying out of focus
- Unplanned multitasking
- Improper prioritization to tasks
- Constant interruptions by phone, e-mail, SMS or person
- Poorly structured routine of work
- Ineffective software that doesn't conform to the natural way in which humans function

Information Fatigue Syndrome (IFS)
Tired? Bewildered?? Confused???

Dr. David Lewis of the International Stress Management Association coined the phrase "Information fatigue syndrome (IFS)" (*http://www.gdrc.org/icts/i-overload/infoload.html*), which is another by-product of "Information overload". The symptoms include paralysis of analytical capacity, increased anxiety, greater self-doubt, and a tendency to blame others. When people are faced with more information than they can process, they become unable to make decisions or take action. This situation creates a new problem, which is known as "Information fatigue syndrome (IFS)". It is a serious problem and it is getting worse by the day. Information overload on the World-Wide Web (WWW) is a well recognized problem. The information, instead of helping to increase productivity, all too often leads to loss of productivity. Research to subdue this problem and extract maximum benefit from the Internet is still in its infancy. With huge amounts of information connected to the Internet, efficient and effective discovery of resource and knowledge has become an imminent research issue. A vast array of networks services is growing up around the

Internet and massive amounts of information are added everyday. Despite the potential benefits of existing indexing, retrieving and searching techniques in assisting users in the browsing process, little has been done to ensure that the information presented is of a high recall and precision standard. Therefore, search for specific information on this massive and exploding information resource base becomes highly critical.

Today, Googling is the prime apparatus in our daily information seeking exercise. We do not always meet our proper destination through Google, but follow some zigzag hocky-pocky to be lost in the deep forest eventually. The phenomenon of "Information Fatigue Syndrome" is the ultimate result of our "Out-of-focus" state. This syndrome is the direct result of the information revolution. Dr. Lewis also emphasized on the symptoms which include the paralysis of the analytical capacity, constant searches for more information, increased anxiety and sleeplessness, as well as increasing self-doubt in decision-making. Information overload is gradually tending to the point of information pollution which leads to the contamination of a culture or of a person's life by excessive data. Another interesting dimension of Information Fatigued Syndrome is "Disposophobia", i.e. the fear of throwing things out. Sometimes we download enormous materials and dump on the disk, without judging whether they are relevant to my subject concerned or not. Our thinking is often smudged by illogical ideas that perhaps I need entire bit of information from the web. Such thinking creates fear of loosing information in our mind. Before start downloading, we have to chalk out our information requirement profile very clearly. Our music library often contains thousands of music tracks and full of movies. We frequently preserve enormous e-mail addresses and social networking accounts that hard to track. These are all positive symptoms of disposophobia.

There are several aspects of "Information overload" problem.

- The first one is information overload due to overwhelming complexity of the situation. Typical examples include network troubleshooting, complex programming and/or networking problem when complexity of the stuff is above human capacity to comprehend. Humor and wit are one of the most affecting methods of fighting stress and overload. They help a person to remain positive in difficult situations.
- The second situation is "junk" information overload when civilization produces more information than necessary for normal functioning, with most information of low quality. This is kind of new type of pollution, *information smog.*
- The third situation is "information overload" due to "channels" problem, i.e. we often use the wrong channels for a given purpose. Email is the most prone to abuse.
- The fourth situation is "information overload" due to poor work management practices. In many IT organizations, the IT managers spend much of their day sending and responding to email messages that actually produce no result. In many academic institutions students spend study time by SMS and e-mail chatting. Cultures of broken work-flow processes automated by email are developing workers with low productivity and low quality who don't have the time to think, read, or learn.
- The fifth situation is "Information overload" due to lack of standardization of keywords. We often designate a particular concept or object with so many keywords and use unnecessary jargons. Use of so many synonymous keywords makes the situation more complex. Let's call a spade a spade

to avoid information overload. It is better to consult any standard vocabulary control. Usage of improper keyword(s) has fostered poorly retrievable systems and created a vicious cycle leading to yet more emails and aimless roaming through web world.

- The sixth situation is "Information overload" due to using keywords without having any knowledge about them. The keywords are ever-changing entities. Very few keywords in any subject-domain are steady, but maximum keywords are ephemeral. The steadiness of keywords can be checked from the indexing/abstracting literature over certain time span.

Information Overload!!!

The phenomenon of proliferation of subjects is perhaps the forerunner of information overload, which was started out as a liberating stream in the post-industrial society, but has turned into a deluge of chaos in the knowledge society. The proliferation of subjects results in growth in publication and printing in all disciplines, which in turn causes information explosion. More experimentation creates more information, causing downpour of torrents of bytes to turn a particular discipline into avalanche of specific subjects. More specific subjects mean more proliferation and more information, to turn eventually in more publications. The number of publications from India had been stable at around 15,000 papers per year until 2000, when there was a prominent upturn in the beginning of this century (Figure 6.1). In the last five years, it increased to just over 25,000 papers per year. This is a 45 per cent increase. The impact of this research has also been increasing over this time as illustrated by the citation rate of Indian research publications (Figure 6.2). From the late 1980's onwards, the citations received by Indian publications have increased constantly (Figure 6.2). Research papers from India received 256,253 citations in the last five years; this is four times as many citations as received in early 1980's. India is also experiencing a rapid increase in patenting activity. Applications have risen from around 10,000 per annum to 24,505 for the financial year 2005-2006, a growth of 40 per cent over the previous financial year 2004-2005. Not only has the volume of innovation increased dramatically, the technologies had also changed significantly in recent times. A ranking of the Top 10 patent assignees for all Indian inventions from 1968 to 2004 (Table 6.1) shows the Council of Scientific and Industrial Research (CSIR) dominating the table, with the rest being headed by Hindustan Lever and Hoechst with its Indian subsidiary Hoechst India. The ranking for 2006 shows CSIR still features as a major innovator in India, though ranked second (Table 6.2), but Microsoft has emerged from nowhere as the most prolific applicant of Indian patents during 2006. This is consistent with the December 2005 announcement of a USD1.7 billion investment by Microsoft in India.

There were 214 daily newspapers published in India during 1950s, which reached 2856 in 1990 and more than 4000 in 2005. Newspaper sale in India has increased by more than 12% in 2008. By 2007, 62 of the world's best selling newspaper dailies were published in China, Japan, and India. India consumed 99 million newspaper copies as of 2007— making it the second largest market in the world for newspapers. There are also more than 50,000 new book titles published every year and, over 60 billion pieces of advertising junk mail come into people's mail boxes every year. Everything from telegraphy and photography in the 19th century to the silicon chip in the twentieth has amplified the stream of information, until matters have reached such proportions today that for the average person, information no longer has any relation to the solution of problems. We have to regularly throw out magazines that are hardly opened. Email overload and its ultimate manifestation, email spam can now be effectively controlled by technical means.

Information Overload
Growth of Information → Growth of Junk Information

The barrage of data, which we are constantly exposed to, carries a cost, both physically and mentally. David Shenk cites psychological studies spanning thirty years and lists several of the symptoms which accompany information overload (Source: http://www.gdrc.org/icts/i-overload/infoload.html):

- Increased cardiovascular stress, due to a rise in blood pressure,
- Weakened vision, citing a Japanese study which predicts a nearly universal near-sightedness in the close future,
- Confusion and frustration,
- Impaired judgement based upon overconfidence,

Researchers at Israel's Tel Aviv University studied 76 electronics industry clerks and found that the sense of relaxation and happiness derived from a vacation began to fade only three days after returning to work. Pre-vacation levels of stress and burn-out returned within a mere three weeks (*Journal of Applied Psychology*, August 1997). For those who remain "in touch" via pagers, cell phones, laptops, radio, and TV, the results will be even more dismal. On a society-wide level, the dangers of information overload are enormous. The engendered feelings of helplessness, confusion, and anger will erode work efficiency, family functioning, and most likely increase crime rates. We will lack the information-processing skills needed to elect responsible leaders or counter the myriad waves of propaganda pushing our money this way and that. The effective ways of information processing and organisation only can make a control over such chaotic situation.

Besides, another major cause of information overload is the ignorance about information need. The majority of information seekers don't know what they actually want, or what their proper need is. On the other hand, a large number of information seekers can't express their need through a suitable keyword, or keyphrase. The choice of most suitable keyword is the major criteria to increase precession of information retrieval results and to reduce junk information minimizing information overload simultaneously. We need some logical models for selection of most appropriate keyword from the large ocean of information of a subject.

SIX DO'S AND SIX DON'TS TO OVERCOME OVERLOAD

Do's

- To develop an information management strategy that is helpful for us.
- To filter information.
- To recognize relevant and quality data for processing.
- To take control over information by ourselves, but absolutely not the reverse.
- To decide topic before starting surfing net.
- To select core keywords of the concerned topic for a stream lined surfing.

Don'ts

- Not to surf internet more than 35 hours per week.
- Not to surf internet aimlessly. Aimless surfing mislays the right destination. We are lost in the forest of sites.
- Not to go through entire messages in cell phones and mailbox.
- Not to attempt to examine every piece of data available.
- Not to focus on things beyond our control, such as the number of new Web pages being added daily.
- Not to be addicted in internet. It is incorrect to spend time in surfing at the cost of other routine engagements, which we often do.

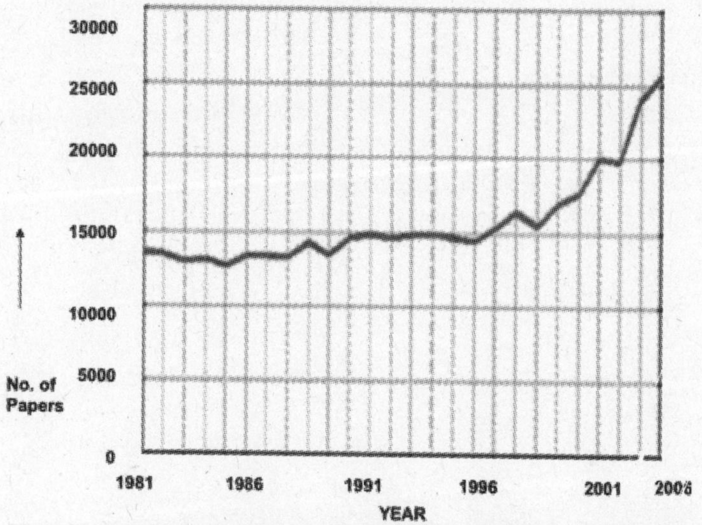

Fig. 6.1: Research papers published in India covering all subject fields from 1981 to 2006

***Source*: Bob Stembridge, Thomson Scientific Press Release, November, 2007 (http://science.thomsonreuters.com/i/klnl/8418376/indiafig1.gif)**

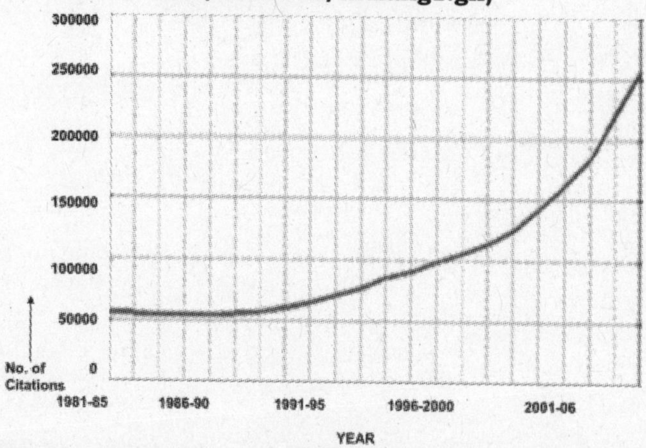

Fig. 6.2 : Number of citations received by the research papers published in India Covering all subject fields from 1981 to 2006

***Source*: Bob Stembridge, Thomson Scientific Press Release, November, 2007 (http://scientific.thomsonreuters.com/news/2007-11/8418387/)**

Table 6.1 : Top 10 assignees for Indian patent publications, 1968-2004

Rank	Assignee/Applicant	Number of Indian patents	Number of patents overall	%tage of total patents
1	COUNCIL SCIENT IND RES (CSIR)	3083	8510	36.22
2	HINDUSTAN LEVER LTD	946	3511	26.94
3	HOECHST	766	170375	0.45
4	SIEMENS AG	685	498690	0.14
5	WESTINGHOUSE ELECTRIC CORP	477	131175	0.36
6	UNION CARBIDE CORP	365	62677	0.58
7	PROCTER & GAMBLE	337	108401	0.31
8	RIETER AG MASCHF	336	8649	3.88
9	LUCAS IND PLC	326	31280	1.04
10	ICI PLC	308	100722	0.31

Source: Bob Stembridge, Thomson Scientific Press Release, November, 2007 (http://scientific.thomsonreuters.com/news/2007-11/8418387/)

Table 6.2 : Top 10 assignees for Indian patent publications, 2006

Rank	Assignee/Applicant	Number of Indian patents	Number of patents overall	%age of total patents
1	MICROSOFT CORP	584	15223	3.84
2	COUNCIL SCIENT IND RES	476	2152	22.12
3	JOHNSON & JOHNSON	271	3691	7.34
4	QUALCOMM INC	249	3779	6.59
5	HONDA MOTOR CO LTD	237	45350	0.52
6	SAMSUNG ELECTRONICS	216	126996	0.17
7	KONINK PHILIPS ELECTRIC	194	23008	0.84
8	THOMSON LICENSING SA	157	3263	4.81
9	HINDUSTAN LEVER LTD	146	2238	6.52
10	MOTOROLA INC	145	23193	0.63

Source: Bob Stembridge, Thomson Scientific Press Release, November, 2007 (http://scientific.thomsonreuters.com/news/2007-11/8418387/)

7
Information Control

Information management is the heart and soul of an information system. An information system functions smoothly if fuelled by right information in right amount at right time to the right clientele, whereas an excess of noisy information creates hindrance to the easy progress of the said system. A system needs an effective information control strategy to avoid noisy information. Today we have copious flow of information, but only a trifle bit is useful to us. Being flooded with information does not mean we are receiving right information in right amount at right time from the right person; rather we get stuffed with junk information. That's why we need proper information control strategy. Information Management helps us to deliver any type of structured or unstructured data that is integrated, accurate and punctual. There are so many meanings of information management. Some definitions are collected from Google and given below:

- IM is the means by which an organisation maximizes the efficiency with which it plans, collects, organizes, uses, controls, stores and disseminates (www.quantum3.co.za/CI%20Glossary.htm)
- The procedure of collecting data and processing, presenting and communicating information (en.

wikibooks.org/wiki/SA_NCS_Computer_Application_Technology:Glossary)

- The provision of relevant information to the right person at the right time in a usable form to facilitate situational understanding and decision making. It uses procedures and information systems to collect, process, store, display, and disseminate information. (https://rdl.train.army.mil/soldierPortal/atia/adlsc/view/public/7422-1/fm/3-13/glos.htm;jsessionid=MvnFH3yTHgWVsbGdH1zbk0Jyx82JCpBghJJ lnpvwQhY51vkgrgQQ !74318302)
- The planning, budgeting, manipulating, and controlling of information throughout its life cycle (www.stanlake.co.uk/recruitment-candidates/recruitment-glossary.php)
- The entire process of defining, evaluating, protecting, and distributing data within an organization (www.storsoftcorp.com/Glossary.htm)
- IM is the collection and management of information from one or more sources and the distribution of that information to various recipients (en.wikipedia.org/wiki/Information management)

According to Albert Einstein (1879-1955), "There are only two ways to live your life. One is as though nothing is a miracle. The other is as though everything is a miracle." Just like the "Ancient Mariner's" groan, "Water, water, everywhere/ Nor any drop to drink", today's miracle is, information is everywhere, but not a bit to hit. This miracle alters basic ways of our lifestyle. We are constantly drowning in information, while an exact bit remaining untouched. The information explosion phenomenon adds new dimension to the concept of information management that is the ways to get rid from information and data overload. Some key steps that can be taken for managing the data are listed below:

- To classify data for processing in accordance with the need
- To identify critical data for archiving, which have long-lasting significance
- To assess timeliness of data
- To formulate strategy for storage
- To empower users using self-retrieval options for restoration/access
- To monitor type of files being stored

The prime function of information control should be to screen out unreliable information, word pollution, redundancy and irrelevance. Some key steps to weed out irrelevant information are:

- To identify material worthy for attention
- If possible, it is better to get services from the agencies which provide articles on specific areas from different magazines and newspapers. This will save a considerable amount of time and energy
- To develop the strategy for discarding the unworthy
- Not to keep back issues of magazines. The copies of relevant and worthy articles can only be separately filed and preserved
- The Internet is a time waster if the time-management strategy is not known. We usually start searching for something in a site, then follow the links to other related sites and from there follow the links to others and so on ... and before we realize, we must have spend hours on the net. So we have to set a specific time, say 1 hour, before starting our research and stop when the time is over.
- To stay focused on the subject we are searching for
- Not to jump to other links just because they appear to be interesting. Non-stop galloping from this link to that link hazes the destination eventually

- Before starting research for a particular subject on the Net, it is better to spend some time with a paper and pencil prior to get connected. The scientific way is to write down the possible keywords that we are going to search and to write down the URLs of all the sites that we are going to visit. Searching should be done using a good search engine like Google, which is the best for the search using the keywords. Another time-saving technique during Net-surfing is to download or save the documents to the local hard disk and review them off-line. This will save a lot of time and money.

In order to process mass amounts of information, we need to identify noise first. RSS feeds spliced with links from del.icio.us, or extraneous information on FriendFeed, Newsfeed and Webfeed are the possible solutions to some extent. RSS allows users to easily keep track of news from multiple web sites because updates are delivered directly to them. But the problem many people face is that there are so many sources of information that they are trying to keep track of. Information overload is a real problem for many web users, and one way to cope with it is to filter their RSS feeds so one can only see what he or she wants to see. To get back in control, the noise is also to be structured. Otherwise it is difficult to separate noisy information from right information. Addiction to social media is another common practice today. These tools pull our attention. For many people, these distractions are overpowering. No matter the time commitment, social media addicts spend entire chunks of their day online playing with the new, shiny internet toys. Sometimes people spend 10 hours per day online, immersed in the web and social media tools. It seems we are at a crossroads. There's so much information, but not enough filters.

Before looking for information on any topic, it is necessary to make some decisions about what we are looking for. The following checklist may help in this regard:

- What we need? Books or periodical articles or both? Periodical articles will give more up-to-date information in science areas
- Do we need current or historical information?
- How much information we want? A few good articles or everything that has ever been written on a subject?
- How much time do we have?
- What level of information do we want? Serious and scholarly, popular, state-of-the-art, report, more newsy, or written for the non-specialist e.g. an encyclopedia article?
- What we do not want?
- What keywords will be used in a search?

Selection of keywords is a crucial aspect. The major cause of noisy information is due to choosing inappropriate keywords. Suitable keywords can increase precision in a retrieval function. Noise is reduced in a system having enhanced precision value. The concept of Information Filtering (IF) has recently gained momentum. According to Beerud Dilip Sheth (http://agents.media.mit.edu/publications/sheth-thesis.pdf), there are three approaches of information filtering systems; viz. cognitive, social or economic. Cognitive systems choose documents based on the characteristics of their contents. Social systems select documents based on the recommendations and annotations of other users and Economic systems select documents based on some computation of cost-benefit to the user and through some pricing mechanisms. According to Humboldt State University Library (Source: http://library.humboldt.edu/~ccm/fingertips/infofilter.html), 5 essential steps to constructing a personal information filter are:

1. List your central life roles:

- spouse
- parent
- career person
- ?

2. List any special hobbies or interests that bring you joy:
   - basket ball
   - gardening
   - jazz
   - tole painting
   - ?
3. List necessary (if not joyful) topics where you need basic and current information:
   - health & medical
   - financial planning
   - ?
4. Now, specify your information needs for each role/ interest:
   - Are your children toddlers or teenagers?
   - If you're an attorney, do you specialize in intellectual property law or criminal defense?
   - Do you grow Iris or Bonsai?
   - Are you especially interested in financial planning to buy your first home or your retirement mansion on the golf course?
5. Next, invest the time to select the 1-3 best periodicals or online sources for each interest or role.
   - Faithfully scan these sources for important-to-you information
   - As you encounter information from other sources, attend to it only to the degree that it matches your interests.

- If material is relevant to your interests, is it an essential piece of information or is it merely desirable?
- Think of all information in relation to how closely it matches the target of your interests.

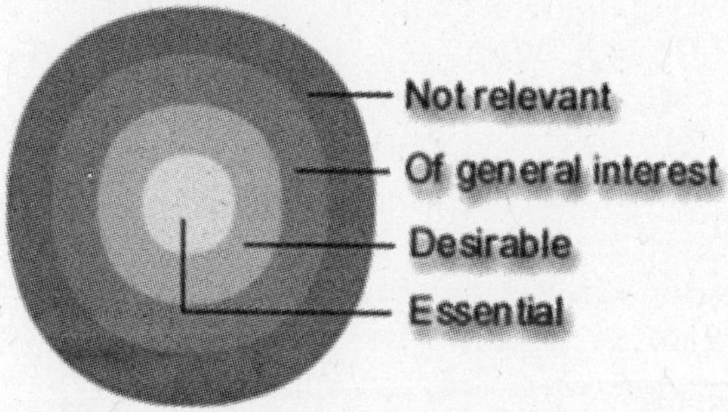

Some major channels of information on Internet are mailing lists, bulletin boards, newsgroups etc. The messaging networks distribute the message to each of the members of the group. The average effort of writing a simple message is about four minutes, and the average effort of reading a message is about half a minute. So if there are more than about eight recipients to a message, the total reading time is larger than the total writing time, and if there are hundreds or thousands of recipients, the total reading time caused by the originator is many times larger than his effort in writing the message. Because of this, Internet users will easily become overloaded with messages (Denning 1982, Palme 1984, Hiltz and Turoff 1985, Malone 1987). Information filters are more important for group messages (messages sent to mailing lists and forums) than for individually addressed mail.

Some major filtering methods:

Automatic filtering : In this method the computer evaluates information.

Social filtering (also known as collaborative filtering) : This is the tool where groups of people help individuals to evaluate information. The social filtering assigns some kind of ratings to documents and/or information. Social filtering has some similarities to the filtering done by editors, journalists and publishers, since in both cases humans select the filtering attributes. It is difficult to design automatic or intelligent filtering algorithms which really can evaluate the content of a document. Humans are more capable of really deciding the value of a document. The simplest and most common filtering is by organizing discussions into groups (newsgroups, mailing lists, forums, etc.). Each group has a topic and wants contributions only from that topic. Sometimes the right to submit contributions is restricted. A common convention is that only members can submit, and sometimes competence control is done before accepting a new member. Another strategy is that special moderators must approve contributions before distribution. The act when a recipient selects which groups to subscribe to, can thus be seen as an act of setting a personal filter. If a social filtering database stores information for individual raters, then that information may be used for infringement of privacy. Some encryption method should be used to make such invasion impossible or difficult. This will of course depend on trust between user and filtering service. Web search engines today can store information about what we search for on the web. They also use this information to target selection for advertisements and other uses, which one may not like.

Filtering by threads : Another simple and common filtering method is to filter by thread. A thread is a stream of inter-related messages. People can use threads for filtering by specifying that whether they want to skip reading of existing and future contributions in certain threads or not. In discussion groups, messages often belong to threads. It may then not be possible to understand a single message without seeing other messages in the same thread. A filter or search facility which only selects certain individual messages, out of threads, might then not satisfy their users. The filter must either select several items in the thread, or at least make it very easy for users, when reading one selected message, to traverse the tree up and down from this message.

Intelligent filtering : This is the use of artificial intelligence (AI) methods to enhance filtering. AI software can derive attributes for documents, which are then used for filtering. With the machine learning approach, the filter will take as input information from the user about which documents the user likes, and will then derive common characteristics of them to be used in future filtering. Such filtering can be done in the background, behind the scenes, with little or no interaction with the user. A disadvantage with much user interaction is that it takes user time, while the whole idea of filtering is to save user time. The user may not trust a filter if he does not understand how it works.

Filtering against spamming : Spamming is the ways in which people can cheat the system to force messages on us which we do not want. Spamming can also be done against Internet search engines. Authors of web documents sometimes assign faulty keywords to their documents, to cheat the search engine into selecting the document by inserting the most popular search terms, just like the words "sex", "naked", "girl", etc., even if these words are not related to the actual content of the document. Some search engines will first show the documents which contain the search word many times, so spammers may repeat the same word many times in the keyword set. The keywords are placed in the meta fields of HTML documents, which is not shown when we read the document with a web browser. Search engine providers have developed methods to recognize and dismiss messages with such false keywords. If social filtering systems are used in the future, there is an obvious risk that spammers will try to cheat the system, by entering lots of false positive ratings of their web pages. To stop this, some kind of authentication of raters may be needed. Sometimes we need filters also for removal of unwanted marketing or propagandist e-mail messages. To do this, the filter has to recognize special properties of spam messages, which distinguish them from other messages. Examples of such properties are:

1. A message does not have our name or e-mail address in the message heading, but it does not come from any mailing list, which we subscribe to. Many, but not all, such messages are spams.
2. The author or sender of a message may have an illegal e-mail address. Many e-mail servers now stop such messages, and because of this, the spammers have started to use legal e-mail addresses as senders. This is a general problem. If a particular filtering method gets very much used, spammers will change their messages to avoid being filtered.
3. Certain words, such as "money" or "$$$" in the subject are not dependable.
4. After frequent receiving of similar spams, we have to recognize special properties of them to use to stop further similar spams.

The question of information security and also maintenance of privacy of information for individuals is thus a vital point for all variants of filtering.

The possible steps towards an effective information control management may also include following steps (Source: *Fighting data asphyxiation is difficult but possible* ... by William Van Winkle; Collected from a website: http://www.gdrc.org/icts/i-overload/infoload.html):

1. At the office

- Be careful with your phone time. Leave a short, efficient message which indicates precisely what action you want to be taken.

- Reduce paper. Either use and file it or toss it in the recycle bin. There is no paper involved, and the "delete" key really can be your best friend.
- Get organized. Corel CENTRAL or Microsoft's Outlook are good examples of utilities which will structure your time.
- Keep meetings short, sweet, and focused.

2. At home

- Reduce television time. Television programme are mostly fluffing designed more to sell commercials than to educate the public. Commercials now account for half of each hour's broadcast.
- Keep your phone number unlisted to reduce solicitation calls.
- Prioritize your phone time. Its taken years, but friends and family have learned to call me with planned discussion items and then not take it personally when I shove the call to a conclusion.
- Develop a hobby. Many of us feel that we don't have the time or talent for a hobby, or may be that was something our parents did — and God knows we don't want to be like them. A hobby, however, besides having its own inherent rewards (not to mention a second possible source of income) will take time from otherwise wasteful brain drains like TV.

3. On the Net

- E-mail can be a virus in its own right. Only drop your address when essential, because software robots will see it and automatically add you to marketing lists.
- Newsgroups can consume your life. Be aware of them.
- Remember the library when doing research; you

may save innumerable hours forsaking the Web altogether and logging into your local library's server.

An important consequence of information filtering is proper assessment of quality of information. There are several factors which increase the quality of information and give it some added values. These factors are:

- The recipient of information and/or data. The data has to get to the right person, otherwise it will be useless
- Time of arrival. Information at right time is a treasury. Obsolete information in most cases is nothing but a junk.
- The 'resolution' of the information, i.e. how clearly it is expressed
- The consonance between the creator and recipient of information. Otherwise is difficult for the information to be absorbed by the recipient
- The creator of information should have some authentication

Another fruitful way of information control is to build up different types of network in different functional areas by individuals.

Personal network : The information flow in the context of professional career keeps us up-to-date and maintains our level of expertise for occupation. We receive streams of information occasionally that are just wasting time without any positive return to either our personal life, or career. We have to discard the information that has limited value and ephemeral. We have to develop networks with professional colleagues belonging to similar subject areas for regular exchange and updating of information. Only gathering of information is not enough, it is mandatory to share information also. Information gathering can't alone make us info-rich, unless it is being shared. A personal network helps in both gathering and sharing of information.

Core network : If information is being properly organized in the personal network, then it is necessary to build up a core network. The information needed in this network is belonging to core area of interest of the information user.

External network : The next step is external network. As no research or study can progress isolated, it is also necessary to build up a network with the experts from the allied areas of research and/or study in order to get supporting information as and when needed.

These networks reduce the incoming information load and make it manageable. There is, however, by no means a definitive and universal guide to dealing with information control and management. Here is the key to recognizing change without creating information overload. New persons may be added to the network to share information on a regular basis. They will inform new happenings and phenomenal changes. Vast quantities of information may be processed and extracted in this way. The information technology revolution turns books into files and the cyber revolution turns information management into keyword management, as every bit of information is stored in our memory in the form of a keyword or a group of keywords. To memorize a situation or any context, we recall some keyword(s) first. We normally designate any sentiment, or emotion, or any special moment or context, or any particular sense of attachment etc. by one or a set of keyword(s). The viability of keyword analysis is thus potentially considerable. The importance and significance of keywords are highly substantial. All writings begin with a title and most of them include an abstract. Several include 'keywords'. All three of these features describe an article's content with varying degrees of detail and abstraction. The title is designed to stimulate the reader's interest. The abstract summarizes the content. The keywords indicate main concepts and fields of concern. The keywords are also known as 'descriptors' or 'subject headings'; the term 'keyword' appears in common usage, while 'descriptor' should strictly speaking be called 'keywords and phrases', since multiword phrases can be used as descriptors in most publications. The four essential parameters of an article, viz, title, author, abstract and keywords are required in any bibliographic database designed to aid electronic information retrieval. The earliest use of keywords was found in 1975 in the *Journal of Applied Behaviour Analysis.*

Keywords allow readers to decide whether or not an article contains material relevant to their interest. Keywords provide readers with suitable terms to use in web-based searches to locate other materials on similar topics. Keywords also enable indexers and editors to group together related materials. Any subject, whether very specific or broad one, always undergoes through incessant changes, which are very picturesquely reflected from the keywords pertaining to the concerned field. Keywords indicate growth of a subject in different orientations but the notable feature is that selection of keywords is a vital aspect. If the keywords are not selected in concise way but scattered over irrelevant peripheral areas then they will mislead both the information professional and clientele. Keywords occur within titles, abstracts, series names, content notes, subject headings and index terms are supplied by the authors. The keywords may also be used as effective subject access points. It is to be noted that every word in titles, abstract or content-notes are not keywords. Articles, prepositions and conjunctions are too common to serve as keywords. To provide an effective keyword management system, first we need methods to categorize keywords in some groups according to different parameters. In the next two chapters the categorization of keywords has been discussed. Before switching over, some services that allow filter by keyword are presented below.

According to (www.readwriteweb.com), there are six ways to filter RSS feeds:

There are many ways to filter news feeds from your favorite sources, including passively by relying on meme trackers like *Techmeme* or social news services such as Google Reader's shared items. We've also taken a look in the past at automatic filters such as *Feedhub* (*our coverage*) which learns from your behavior to suggest posts, or *AideRSS* (*our coverage* and *here*), which uses outside metrics to determine which items in an RSS feed are the "best." For the purpose of this post, however, we'll focus on services that let you filter by keyword.

Feed Rinse is a best of class RSS filtering application. It offers filtering by keyword, tag, author, title, etc. It supports regular expressions, has a built in profanity filter, and lets you upload your OPML file for easy importing of your RSS feeds (it can also export to OPML). And since we first covered it in *April of 2006* it has gone completely free.

FilterMyRSS is a no-nonsense keyword filter that filters posts out by keyword. By that we mean that the service tracks posts for the keywords you want to filter and removes posts where it finds matches. It can filter by description, title, or category and offers some advanced XML options.

When we *first reviewed* 2or3things' *Blastfeed* in late 2006 it appeared to be shaping up as a good consumer filtering alternative to Feed Rinse. But since, the company has shifted gears and now offers Blastfeed as an enterprise filtering solution. Blastfeed's keyword filters can also be used to remix and republish blog feeds filtered for specific content — for example, a fan site for a specific band could create a news feed from multiple general music sites that publishes only stories about that specific band.

Feed Sifter

Feed Sifter is an almost painfully simple RSS filter that filters in by keyword. Or, in other words, it watches for the keywords you enter and pushes stories to you that match those keywords. It can search for single keywords, or return stories that only match sets of keywords.

ZapTXT

ZapTXT is a keyword filter (of the in variety) that returns results via email, instant messenger, or mobile phone. It is designed for people who prefer to consume RSS feeds via non-traditional methods (i.e., not via an RSS reader). ZapTXT also powers email, IM, and SMS alerts for sites like *TheStreet.com.*

beta pipes™

For do-it-yourselfers, *Yahoo! Pipes* offers an easy way to create filtered RSS feeds. The RSS remixing application makes it easy to create simple filters. Just define your feed using the "Fetch Feed" module, connect it to a "Filter" module, which can filter either in or out by title, description, category, author, or date, and then connect it out to the Pipe Output. It isn't as comprehensive as Feed Rinse, but you do perhaps have more control. The example pipe below would filter our feed and return only posts that talk about "Facebook" in the title.

8

Keyword : The Quantum of Information

KEYWORD ANALYSIS

A keyword is the starter of a search. A keyword is either a single word or a combination of words, but the sense of a keyword is not limited within the domain of just a word. Actually all keywords are word(s), but all words are not keywords. After studying several keywords in different subject areas, it has been observed that in general a keyword can be broken up in three kernels, which are the building blocks of a keyword. These three kernels have been given the names as follows: 1) Keyphrase, 2) Modulator and 3) Qualifier. These building blocks are the kernels of meaning in which the entire keyword has been split up. The keyphrase constitutes the core or nucleus of the concept carried by the whole keyword and manifests the central theme underlying behind the concept, the modulator amends the central theme in accordance with the relevant context. The modulator modulates the manifestation by the total spectrum of the central theme and polarizes the all-pervaded manifestation of the keyphrase in a specific orientation. The modulator constitutes the first level orbital of the core or nucleus. The qualifier comes after the modulator to describe the particular state of the central concept and/or amended concept without disturbing the conceptual wholeness. The qualifier constitutes the second level orbital of the nucleus. It is to be noted that all keywords studied here do not consist of all these three parts. The keyphrase is mandatory, i.e. each and every keyword must have a keyphrase, whereas other two components are optional, i.e. a keyword may or may not contain either a modulator or a qualifier or both. The sequence of outcome of these three components is:

Keyphrase → Modulator → Qualifier. The physical structure of a keyword thus takes the form as given below:

$$\text{Keyword} = \left(\frac{\text{Keyphrase}}{\text{Mandatory}} + \frac{\text{Modulator}}{\text{Optional}}\right), \frac{\text{Qualifier}}{\text{Optional}}$$

This is, actually the generalized structure of a keyword as considered in the present study. In this study, a considerable number of keywords contain only the keyphrase part, and some keywords contain keyphrase and modulator or qualifier. The remaining keywords contain all the three components. The keyphrase is a subject-specific term/terms, the modulator may either be a subject-specific term/terms or a general word/words and the qualifier is a general word for majority of keywords. The qualifier hardly becomes a subject-specific term. Let us now clarify with example as shown in the Table 8.1 below. Here the examples are taken from the subject "Condensed matter physics", but the proposed generalized structure may be applicable to all keywords belonging to any area(s). Nine keywords are shown in Table 8.1 as example. In the keyword, "Fermi-Liquid Transition, Ferromagnetic-Paramagnetic", the core concept is contained in the term "Fermi-Liquid". The term "Fermi-Liquid" is thus the keyphrase of this keyword. The term "Transition" modulates or limits the whole spectrum of concept signaled by the keyphrase "Fermi-Liquid" to a narrow domain. The keyphrase "Fermi-Liquid" indicates a broad area, while "Fermi-Liquid Transition" indicates only a particular aspect of "Fermi-Liquid", i.e. only transitional properties. The term "Transition" is thus the modulator of this keyword. The term "Ferromagnetic-Paramagnetic" describes the particular state of the term "Fermi-Liquid Transition". This term qualifies the term "Fermi-Liquid Transition", and it is an adjective. The qualifiers are adjectives or adverbs in almost all cases. The term "Ferromagnetic-Paramagnetic" is thus the qualifier of this keyword.

The keyphrase, modulator and qualifier – all these three kernels may be formed either by single word or multiple words. The constituting word or words have been called as keyterm. The keyphrase Fermi-Liquid consists of two keyterms, Fermi and Liquid. The keyterm "Fermi" is taken from the surname of the physicist Enrico Fermi, which is a proper noun. The keyterm "Liquid" is a general term, which is a common noun. The conjunction of two keyterms "Fermi" and "Liquid" gives rise to a keyphrase that indicates a subject domain. In this subject, a large number of keyphrases have been formed by conjunction of the name or a part of the name of a scientist and a general term. For instance, keywords like "Fermi-Liquid", "Kondo-Effect", Luttinger-Liquid", "Hubbard-Model", "Hall-Angle", "Gutzwiller-Theory" etc. are formed in this way. The terms like "Fermi", "Kondo", "Luttinger", "Hubbard", "Gutzwiller" and "Hall" are parts of the names of the concerned scientists; and "Liquid", "Effect", "Model", "Theory" and "Angle" are general terms. The keyterms forming modulators generally describe some phenomenon, entity, group or set. In the examples shown in the Table 8.1, the modulators "Transition", 'Resonance" and "Scattering" describe some phenomenon. The modulator "Phase" is an entity and the modulator "Compound" indicates a set of materials. The keyterms forming qualifiers are general terms in most cases, and subject-specific terms in few cases. In the examples shown in the Table 8.1, the qualifiers "Multiparticle", "Incoherent", "Local" and "Chaotic" are general terms. The qualifiers "Ferromagnetic-Paramagnetic", "Excitonic" and "Isoelectronic" are subject-specific terms. The qualifier "Tomonaga" is a part of the name of a scientist and describes a particular state of the keyphrase "Luttinger-Liquid". Non-adjectives or non-adverbs may also be qualifiers. For instance, in the keyword "Fermi-Liquid Resonance, Multiparticle", the qualifier is "Multiparticle", which is not an adjective or adverb, but a noun. The keywords "Luttinger-Liquid, Local Tomonaga" and "Quantum-Dot, Chaotic" have no modulator, but only keyphrase and qualifier; while the keywords "Neutrino-Nucleon Scattering" has no qualifier, but only keyphrase and modulator. The keywords "Hall-Angle" and "Gutzwiller-Theory" contain only keyphrase, but no modulator or qualifier.

Table 8.1 : Examples of three kernels of keywords

Keyword	*Keyphrase*	*Modulator*	*Qualifier*
Fermi-Liquid Transition, Ferromagnetic-Paramagnetic	Fermi-Liquid	Transition	Ferromagnetic-Paramagnetic
Fermi-Liquid Resonance, Multiparticle	Fermi-Liquid	Resonance	Multiparticle
Fermi-Liquid Phase, Incoherent Excitonic	Fermi-Liquid	Phase	Incoherent Excitonic
Kondo-Lattice Compound, Isoelectronic	Kondo-Lattice	Compound	Isoelectronic
Luttinger-Liquid, Local- Tomonaga	Luttinger-Liquid	X	Local- Tomonaga
Quantum-Dot, Chaotic	Quantum-Dot	X	Chaotic

Keyword	*Keyphrase*	*Modulator*	*Qualifier*
Neutrino-Nucleon Scattering	Neutrino-Nucleon	Scattering	X
Hall-Angle	Hall-Angle	X	X
Gutzwiller-Theory	Gutzwiller-Theory	X	X

9
Keyword Categories

The keywords may be categorized in different classes on the basis of different parameters as listed below. Here sixteen unique categories are considered on the basis of four fundamental properties of a keyword. The cross-categorization among different categories belonging to different properties is also possible. The categories under same property can't overlap. The four properties of the keywords are:

1) Mode of association or Associativeness with the subject-content (3)
2) Chronological appearance (4)
3) Frequency of occurrence (3) and
4) Category (6)

The figures within right-side first brackets indicate number of unique categories under the corresponding property. The number of unique categories is 3+4+3+6 =16; and total number of cross-categorized classes is 3*4*3*6=216. There are both popular and scholarly keywords as well. A sample (17945 in number) of scholarly keywords were collected from different journal articles on Condensed Matter Physics over a specific span of time (1985-2004) and then categorized in accordance with the above-mentioned scheme (Dutta, B 2008). It was observed that the majority of keywords occurred in flocks or groups. Some keywords grouped in to form very large clusters, while some other formed medium-sized clusters and a considerable number of keywords formed tiny clusters. The cluster-forming keywords possess identical keyphrase, but different modulator(s) and/or qualifier(s), as the case may be. Any cluster therefore has only one keyphrase, and it is introduced by the name of the keyphrase; that is the keyphrase and the cluster hold an identical name. Maximum clusters are very small in size and few clusters are very large in size. The keywords forming clusters have been categorized as 'clustered keywords', which is further classified in three sub-groups depending on their associativeness to the subject concerned, viz. core cluster, allied cluster and alien cluster. The identification of clusters has been executed on the basis of the number of keywords they contain. The total number of clustered keywords has been partitioned in three equal segments containing equal number of keywords. The first segment of keywords contain a few clusters, which are termed as "core cluster"; the second segment of keywords are scattered over larger number of clusters, and termed as "allied cluster"; whereas the third segment of keywords are scattered over largest number of clusters, which are termed as "alien cluster". The core clusters are large in size as they contain large number of keywords and, naturally closely assembled with the central subject-content. The allied clusters are medium in size and contain smaller number of keywords. The allied clusters are moderately relevant to the main subject content. The alien clusters are almost irrelevant to the main subject-content and very small in size. A number of keywords form a couple of two keywords with an identical keyphrase, which are termed as "twin keywords". The third set of keywords occurs in single, which are termed as 'single keywords'. The keyphrase is a common factor within a set of clustered keywords, though the modulator and qualifier vary, and thus the name of each cluster is given in the name of the corresponding keyphrase. The large keyword clusters represent major keyphrases involved in the subject concerned. Keyword cluster analysis (KCA) is a very effective methodology to reckon potential keyphrases of a subject.

The classification with respect to the chronological appearance of the keywords divides the keyword in two groups, i.e. ephemeral keyword and non-ephemeral keyword; while the keywords falling under latter group may further be sub-divided in three sub-groups, i.e. new keyword, stable keyword and obsolete keyword. The explanation of this mode of categorization is given in the Table 9.1.

The alphabets A, B, C etc. represent keywords. The year under consideration is represented by Y. The ephemeral keywords for the year Y occur only in the year Y, whereas the non-ephemeral keywords occur in other years also. If any keyword occurs all other years except the year Y, then it will not be considered as the keyword of the year Y. The keywords A, C are 'New' with respect to the year Y, whereas they are 'Stable' with respect to the year Y+1; similarly, the keywords H, I are 'Stable' with respect to the year Y-1, but 'Obsolete' with respect to the year Y. The classifications new, obsolete and stable are thus temporal classifications, i.e. classifications based on time and hence change from year to year. Today's new keyword may become tomorrow's stable and day-after-tomorrow's obsolete keyword.

The keywords are divided in three groups with respect to its frequency of occurrence over the span of twenty years, i.e. Mono-frequent keyword (keywords having frequency of occurrence one during 1985-2004, i.e. the keyword appeared only one time in one journal-article. It is also clear that all mono-frequent keywords

Table 9.1: Ephemeral and Non-Ephemeral Keywords (Definition)

Keyword-type \ *Year*		*Y-2*	*Y-1*	*Y (Concerned Year)*	*Y+1*	*Y+2*	*Total*
Non-Ephemeral	New			A, B, C	A, C	A, B	w
	Stable	D, E, F	D, F	D, E, F	E, F	D, E	l
	Obsolete	G, H, I	H, I	G, H, I			b
Ephemeral				J, K, L			e
Total							n

are also ephemeral according to the criteria of chronological appearance as defined in Table 9.2), Di-frequent keyword (keywords having frequency two, i.e. the keyword appeared either once in two journal-articles, or two times in one journal-article at each instant) and Multi-frequent keyword (keywords having frequencies larger than two).

Lastly, the keywords are divided in six groups with respect to its categories, i.e. Action, Theory, Entity, Material, Property and Method. The elementary category Action indicates some sort of work or function to express the concept of "Doing". Action may be categorized as Self-action and External-action. The examples of self-action are emission, condensation, decay etc. and calculation, collaboration, scaling etc. are external actions. The category Theory reflects the micro and macro conceptual organization of an idea in the concerned subject. The examples are: approximation theory, Kondo effect, Hubbard model etc. The keywords expressing some model or parameter are also included in the scope of this category. The category Entity include manifestations having perceptual correlates, or having only conceptual existence, as contrasted with their properties and actions performed by them or on them, for example, "Fermi-Liquid Ground-State, Highly-Anisotropic" etc. The scope of this category includes energy, light, plant, living and non-living being, place, time etc. The category Material represents the focal idea of the subject involved. The focal idea spots the central theme of the subject. The examples are: Alloy-Compound, Electron-Accelerator etc. The category Property indicates the concept of "Attribute" or "Quality". The scope of the category Property includes effect, form, capability, utility etc. The examples are: angular asymmetry, axial anomaly etc. The category Method indicates some ways of any execution or performance, any sort of procedural concept etc. The examples are: constant photocurrent method, self-flux method etc.

The classification of keywords with respect to its Associativeness with the subject-content helps in providing content-description and in executing content analysis of a Subject. The chronological appearance of keywords reveals about obsolescence and recency of research on a subject. The frequency of occurrence of keywords reflects the intensity of research on a topic. The impact of a subject with universe of knowledge is well understood from different categories of keywords. The cross-classification among different categories of keywords is plausible and the cross-classification creates 216 classes (As 3*4*3*6 = 216) based on the taxonomy scheme given below. The keywords can be placed in different classes, where each class indicates a particular aspect of research. The semantic relation among the keywords may be understood, and the core keywords can also be obtained to identify thrust areas of research. The core keywords are effective means to develop an efficient subject access tool. The new taxonomy of keywords is presented in Table 9.2.

The clustered keywords may further be classified in three zones: core cluster, allied cluster and alien cluster. Each of these three classes may be split up in different levels. Here only three levels for core cluster and two levels for each of the other two clusters have been mentioned, as in the present study more than 95% clustered keywords have not more than two levels. For instance, let us take the following four keywords as an example:

Spin Wave Damping

Spin Wave Damping, Transverse

Spin Wave Damping, Zero Temperature

Spin Wave Damping, Zero Temperature Polarization-Induced

Here, the keyphrase is "Spin", which is the basic subject and one of the core clusters of the subject 'Fermi

Table 9.2 : Keyword Taxonomy

<table>
<tr><th>Major criteria for classification of keywords</th><th>No. of classified keyword clusters</th><th colspan="2">Name of each cluster</th></tr>
<tr><td rowspan="3">Mode of Association or Associativeness with the Subject-Content (ASC)</td><td rowspan="3">3</td><td colspan="2">Clustered</td></tr>
<tr><td colspan="2">Twin</td></tr>
<tr><td colspan="2">Single</td></tr>
<tr><td rowspan="4">Chronological Appearance (CAP)</td><td rowspan="4">4</td><td colspan="2">Ephemeral</td></tr>
<tr><td rowspan="3">Non-Ephemeral (F)</td><td>New</td></tr>
<tr><td>Stable</td></tr>
<tr><td>Obsolete</td></tr>
<tr><td rowspan="3">Frequency of Occurrence (FOC)</td><td rowspan="3">3</td><td colspan="2">Mono-frequent</td></tr>
<tr><td colspan="2">Di-frequent</td></tr>
<tr><td colspan="2">Multi-frequent</td></tr>
<tr><td rowspan="6">Category (CAT)</td><td rowspan="6">6</td><td colspan="2">Action</td></tr>
<tr><td colspan="2">Theory</td></tr>
<tr><td colspan="2">Entity</td></tr>
<tr><td colspan="2">Material</td></tr>
<tr><td colspan="2">Property</td></tr>
<tr><td colspan="2">Method</td></tr>
</table>

liquid'. It is the top term. The clustering of the keywords containing the keyphrase 'Spin' is the association at first level. The modulators are "Wave" and "Damping". The words after comma represent qualifiers. The phrase 'Spin wave' represents association at second level. The phrase 'Spin wave damping' represents association at third level, and lastly the phrase 'Spin Wave Damping, Zero Temperature' represents association at fourth level. The Table 9.3 illustrates different levels of association of the keyphrases and the corresponding notations.

Table 9.3: Clustered keyword

Three zones of clusters	*Different levels of association of keyphrases*
Core Cluster (C)	Level-1
	Level-2
	Level-3
	....
AlliedCluster (A)	Level-1
	Level-2
	....
Alien Cluster (N)	Level-1
	Level-2
	....

10
Folksonomy & Tagging

For several decades subject indexing was a common practice within the domain of library and information science, which is only practiced by library and information professionals. Now a similar process is gaining popularity on the web, i.e. collaborative tagging systems (known as "Folksonomy") that allow users to publicly annotate links, photographs, references and other items with keywords or 'tags'. Popular annotation systems like del.ico.us, flickr, technorati, RawSugar, CiteULike, etc. have already reached several million users. They are part of a movement with several web-based services like weblogs, wikis, and peer-to-peer that focus on the communication and interaction between users instead of using the traditional centralized one-to-many model of publication. According to Wikipedia, "Folksonomy (also known as collaborative tagging, social classification, social indexing, and social tagging) is the practice and method of collaboratively creating and managing tags to annotate and categorize content. Folksonomy describes the bottom-up classification systems that emerge from social tagging. In contrast to traditional subject indexing, metadata is generated not only by experts but also by creators and consumers of the content. Usually, freely chosen keywords are used instead of a controlled vocabulary. Folksonomy (from folk + taxonomy) is a user-generated taxonomy". The term "Folksonomy" (also known as: collaborative tagging; distributed classification system; ethnoclassification; and social bookmarking) was coined by Thomas Vander Wal, who describes it as follows: "Folksonomy is the result of personal free tagging of information and objects (anything with a URL) for one's own retrieval. The tagging is done in a social environment (shared and open to others). The act of tagging is done by the person consuming the information. The value in this external tagging is derived from people using their own vocabulary and adding explicit meaning, which may come from inferred understanding of the information/object as well as. The people are not so much categorizing as providing a means to connect items and to provide their meaning in their own understanding." (<http://www.vanderwal.net/random/ entrysel.php?blog=1750>) In reality, a growing number of web sites employ "social software" to provide a new level of functionality that gives the "user" the ability to assign descriptive words (tags) to "objects" they find or place on the web site. One of the most popular social software sites is Wikipedia, which is an open content encyclopedia that is collaboratively edited by its users. By the end of 2005 there are Wikipedias in more than 200 languages with 2.8 million articles combined. The goal of Wikimedia Foundation (Wikipedia's parent organization) is to provide free access to all human knowledge of the world; beside Wikipedia there is a free media archive (Wikicommons), a repository of free e-books (Wikibooks), a source of News reports (Wikinews), a multilingual dictionary and thesaurus (Wiktionary) and other projects. All of them are collaboratively developed by its users using the MediaWiki software. The content is free under the GNU Free Documentation License (GFDL), meaning that it may be freely used, edited, copied, and redistributed subject to the restrictions of that license.

MediaWiki provides categories that are used to classify articles and other pages in the Wikimedia projects. Assigning categories to Wikipedia articles is a form of collaborative tagging with some particularities. The category system is a thesaurus with hierarchical relationships between tags and the categories can both be added and removed.

Del.icio.us (<http://del.icio.us>) and Flickr (<http://www.flickr.com>) are two of best known current examples of folksonomy, but there are many others. It is a user-based approach. The information professional and clientele assign their own tags. Folksonomy thus develops a grassroots, bottom-up structure, as opposed to the hierarchical, top-down model of traditional taxonomies. The traditional taxonomic classification systems were based on compartmentalization of the universe of knowledge into some limited number of components, and then again segmentizing each component into some more sub-components, then again breaking each sub-component into still more sub(sub-component)s, and so on. A specific topic was reached only by delving more and more into the broad areas. In traditional classification every document is classified with only one (primary) class, while a tagging allows assigning multiple descriptors. Compared to professional indexing there is no directive on how many descriptors to assign to a document in collaborative tagging.

But the modern concept is different. The universe of knowledge is highly dynamic and thus constantly expanding. New topics are blooming continuously. Division of such a dynamic, ever-expanding entity into a limited number of components is not properly justified. The folksonomic approach is user-centric in nature. Here the users assign keywords or tags according to their fields of interest. An integration of a corpus of tags or keywords will take some new shape of any specific subject eventually. This is the most interesting feature of folksonomies, i.e. they reflect the vocabulary of the users, regardless of viewpoint, background, bias, and so forth. Folksonomies may thus be viewed as a democratic system where everyone has the opportunity to contribute and share tags (Kroski, 2006). It is quiet difficult to build up and maintain a sound controlled vocabulary. Standardization of any vocabulary is another Herculean task. An application of controlled taxonomies to the Web is too expensive in terms of development time and of the acute learning needed by the user of the system to adopt the classification scheme (Fichter, 2006; Kroski, 2006; Quintarelli, 2005; Shirky, 2004). A further limitation of taxonomies is that they may become obsolete easily. New concepts or products may emerge that are not yet included in the taxonomy; in comparison, on the other hand folksonomies accommodate easily such new concepts (Fichter, 2006; Mitchell, 2005). Shirky (2004) points out that the advantage of folksonomies is not that they are better than controlled vocabularies, but that they are better than nothing, i.e. they are unique in nature. The notable point of a folksonomy is that it is comprised of terms in a flat namespace, i.e. there is no hierarchy, and no directly specified parent-child or sibling relationships between these terms. There are, however, automatically generated "related" tags, which cluster tags based on common URLs. This is unlike formal taxonomies and classification schemes where there are multiple kinds of explicit relationships between terms. These relationships include things like broader, narrower, as well as related terms. While the folksonomies are simply the set of terms that a group of user's tagged content with, they are not a predetermined set of classification terms or labels.

The key element of folksonomy is the social context developed between the tag and its object. A meaningful example of this social context can be found in Clay Shirky's writings on this topic ("Ontology is Overrated" in http://www.shirky.com/writings/ontology_overrated.html), where he discusses the use of tags such as "movie," "film," and "cinema." Apparently these terms appear to be synonymous, but within the social context, there is a significant difference between what one user might tag a "movie" and another might tag a "film." Vander Wal also identifies two kinds of folksonomies, "broad" and "narrow". In a broad folksonomy, a single object has multiple tags that have been assigned to it by multiple users. In the case of del.icio.us, a user identifies a resource on the web and adds it to his "My Favorites" along with any tags (existing tags or new ones) that he wants to associate with the resource. An additional feature of a broad folksonomy is that as different users assign "tag" to the same resource, the social software keeps track of the number of people who have tagged it and also the tags associated with the object. Also, if a particular user has a similar interest, another user can see what other tags that person has used and may discover additional resources of interest by following those tags. Often social bookmarking sites will display the usage of tags through "tag clouds". The larger the tag's size, the greater use the tag is having at any given point in time.

A narrow folksonomy, on the other hand, focuses on objects that are difficult to find through traditional text searches because of the non-text nature of the object, like photographs, images or graphics. In addition only one person or a few selected people can add tags to the object. At Flickr users can upload, tag, organize, and share photographs. The user uploading the photos and controls the level of access to the photos (e.g., to family and/or friends, or public) and to the tags and notes associated with the photo. Even if other users are given the ability to tag others' photos, the Flickr software doesn't keep track of how many users have tagged a particular photo. So although users can use the tags of others to find photos of interest, they have no idea of how many others have also found those photos and they may or may not be able to add their own tags to those photos. Thus the information professionals may interfere over the concept of users making metadata decisions. In reality, there are both advantages and disadvantages to the practice of folksonomy. The most interesting feature of folksonomies has already mentioned, that they reflect the vocabulary of the users, regardless of viewpoint, background, bias, and so forth. On the contrary, there are so many drawbacks on the folksonomic applications. The major weaknesses is that folksonomies have the problems inherent to all uncontrolled vocabularies, such as ambiguity, polysemy, synonymy, and basic level variation (Fichter, 2006; Golder & Huberman, 2006; Guy & Tomkin, 2006; Mathes, 2004). Different users apply terms to documents in different ways. Thus the terms in a folksonomy may have inherent ambiguity. For instance, let us consider the following two sentences: (1) The house is at the *foot* of the mountains and (2) One of his shoes felt too tight for his *foot.* In the first sentence, '*Foot*' refers to the bottom part of the mountains and in the second sentence "*Foot*" refers to the bottom part of the leg. This is an example of polysemy, where a single keyword carries more than one senses. Similar thing happens when a particular object is tagged by multiple keywords by multiple users. An object may have multiple significances to multiple users and therefore, it is necessary to map links amid all different significances. Here lies the importance of "Domain ontology" to be discussed in next chapter. Also, folksonomies do not include guidelines for use or scope notes. Folksonomies provide for no synonym control; the terms *mac*, *macintosh*, and *apple*, for example, are used to describe Apple Macintosh computers. The keyword "Black hole" is used to describe either the latest stage of stellar evolution or Nawab Siraj-Ud-Doula's agitation against East India Company in history of Bengal. Similarly, both singular and plural forms of terms appear (e.g., flower and flowers), thus creating a number of redundant headings. The problem with basic level variation is that related terms that describe an item vary along a continuum of specificity ranging from very general to very specific; so, for example, documents tagged *apache* and *tomcat* may be too specific for some users, while a document tagged *relational database* may be too general for others. Folksonomies provide no formal guidelines for the choice and form of tags, such as the use of compound headings, punctuation, word order, and so forth; for example, should one use the tag "*Low Temperature*" or "*Temperature, Low*"? In folksonomic space most tags are limited to single words, but there are so many inconsistencies in creating compound words. For example, "social bookmarking" could show up as "socialbookmarking," "social_bookmarking," or "social-bookmarking;" all of which affects search results. The notable advantage is that it is easy for anyone to employ the users' natural language. No structured hierarchies enhance browsability and findability because the terms are bound together, but not free. While in folksonomic space the tags group together resources of interest within a specific social context, which reveals the users' perspective. The tags are potentially responsive to constant changes and new concepts, especially within the realm of blogs and wikis where the content changes continuously, as opposed to static HTML pages.

Some suggestions regarding tag selection were made by Guy and Tomkin (2006), such as the use of plural rather than singular forms or the use of underscore to join terms in a multi-term concept (e.g., developed_ country). But an overall, integrated standardization is needed. The existing subject access tools like Library of Congress Subject Headings or Sear's List of Subject Headings are outmoded to a large extent. These subject access tools were introduced in nineteenth century, and basically provide solutions to nineteenth century problems. These subject access tools and other existing controlled vocabularies like thesaurus and glossaries mainly discuss the inter-term relationships, e.g. hierarchical, associative or equivalent relationship. Now, such relational topologies are not applicable in case of folksonomies, because they contain terms corresponding to choices and other socio-economic and socio-cultural aspects. Another notable point is that an in-depth analysis of the linguistic structure of tags and keywords are also necessary. The terminology-control devices to manage the keywords on the folksonomic space should thus be built up on the basis of effective solutions of these problematic aspects.

FOLKSONOMY: PROS & CONS

Let's have a quick look through.

Pros

- Simple, no complex structure to learn
- Lower cost of categorization
- Open ended – can respond quickly to changes
- Relevance – User's own terms
- Easy to tag any object – photo, document, bookmark
- Making people interested about metadata
- Support unanticipated form of browsing

Cons

- Uncontrolled vocabulary
- Ambiguity in keywords (polysemy & unexpanded acronym)
- Multiple keywords for single concept
- No structure, no conceptual relationships
- Lack of scalability, popular tags are always forerunner
- Limited applicability, only useful for non-technical

or non-specialist domains

- Most people can't tag very well – learned skill
- Errors: misspellings, single words or bad compounds, single use or idiosyncratic use

The Dilemma: Controlled vs. Uncontrolled?

The system of controlled vocabulary is fine, but it may hamper findability. While, browsing the system and its interlinked related tag sets is wonderful for finding things unexpectedly in a general area. Information seeking behavior varies with the expansion of the universe of knowledge and continuous proliferation of subjects. The fundamental question is that how many projects to be undertaken to frame the controlled vocabulary of the entire universe of knowledge. Again, the central area of interest of a user is very specific. Then it is better to let him call his own bit of information, so that he will be able to locate that in the information space, because finding out the desired thing is the actual point. The collaborative tagging system often ignores the standardization activities that the system needs from its structural point of view. It is thus very difficult to say at this time that which one is better. Folksonomy is a topic of active research today in Information science and other related disciplines of social science.

METADATA

The tags in folksonomic space endow with some data. A set of tags belonging to an identical category is represented by another tag, which is known as meta-tag or metadata. Metadata is "Data about data". There are so many definitions of metadata exist now. Some definitions in accordance with Wikipedia are listed below:

- Data about data are referred to as metadata
- Metadata is information about data
- Metadata is information about information

- Metadata contains information about that data or other data

There are more sophisticated definitions, such as:

- Metadata is structured, encoded data that describe characteristics of information-bearing entities to aid in the identification, discovery, assessment, and management of the described entities
- Metadata is a set of optional structured descriptions that are publicly available to explicitly assist in locating objects

From the point of view of creation, metadata may be classified in three classes:

- Metadata created by intellectual contributor (Author)
- Metadata created by information professional (Cataloguer/Indexer)
- Metadata created by information clientele (User)

According to Taylor (2004), there are three broad categories of metadata:

1. Descriptive metadata
2. Structural metadata
3. Administrative metadata

For instance a set of tags like "India", "China", "America" etc. will have a meta-tag or metadata like "Nation" or "Place". There are two creators of metadata (information that describes information): information professionals (such as library catalogers or other professional taxonomists) and information creators (keywords supplied by authors of journal articles or keywords supplied by students submitting electronic theses and dissertations). Professionally-created metadata requires the use of highly trained individuals in the specific system and/or discipline; and consequently this process is labor intensive and relatively expensive. It doesn't scale well when there is a large amount of information to be described. Author-created metadata relies on the skills and integrity of the author to provide the appropriate metadata, and consequently the quality/consistency of the language varies. The evolution of folksonomy brings a third option to the realm of metadata creation, i.e. user-created metadata. One form of explicit user created metadata was popularized in the late 1990's with link-websites called weblogs. These sites provide links combined with commentary, and are a form of mostly unstructured, but explicit, user created metadata. Customer reviews on web sites such as Amazon.com are an integral aspect of online commerce, and leverages consumer created metadata to create sites that are far more informative than comparable commercial sites. The Dublin Core Metadata Initiative has been used with some success in this area.

Some sites on Folksonomy are listed below:

- BBC Backstage Prototype: Social Tagging (<http://bbctags.headshift.com/>): Prototype that gives users the ability to tag BBC news stories.
- CiteULike (<http://www.citeulike.org>): A free service to help academics share, store, and organize the academic papers they are reading.
- Connotea (<http://www.connotea.org/>): A place to keep links to articles read and websites used, and find them again.
- Diigo (<http://diigo.com/>): Social annotation, "write" on and interact with web pages; share marked pages to other services like del.icio.us, Furl, etc.; and use to transfer information to personal blogs.
- Flickr (<http://www.flickr.com>)
- Librarything (<http://www.librarything.com>): An online catalog of personal reading collections.
- Technorati (<http://www.technorati.com/>): A real-time search engine that keeps track of what is going

on in the world of weblogs.

- PennTags (<http://tags.library.upenn.edu/>): A "social bookmarking tool for locating, organizing, and sharing favorite online resources" at the University of Pennsylvania.
- Stuffopolis (<http://www.stuffopolis.com/>): Keeps track of items loaned to friends.
- The Art Museum Social Tagging Project (<http://www.steve.museum/>): "A group of art museums is looking at integrating folksonomies into the museum Web by developing a working prototype for tagging and term collection."

Del.icio.us and Flickr

Del.icio.us (*http://del.icio.us/*) is a tool to organize web pages. It emphasizes on the user added keywords as a fundamental organizational construct. These keywords, which are referred to as "tags" on the site, allow users to describe and organize content with any vocabulary they choose. The system is free to join and use. Only a username, full name, and password are required. The user then adds a specialized bookmark to their web browser. When browsing a web page they would like to add to delicious, they select the bookmark, and are presented with a form that has allows them to enter any tags they want to associate with the page, and then save it. These tags are optional; users can and do use the site without tagging their documents.

Flickr (*http://www.flickr.com/*) is a photo management and sharing web application, has a similar system of free-form tagging for photos that was adopted and modeled after Delicious. It too requires users to create a user account, and is free to join. There is also the option to pay for an account with more features, like more storage space for photographs. Flickr offers a similar bookmark to add photographs to the system, but also has a number of other options to upload photographs to the system through web pages and software applications. Tags can be added at the time of upload, or later in the process when the photographs are displayed by the system.

A primary difference between Delicious and Flickr is that while the tags on Delicious are primarily from the users of web documents that were written by another party, Flickr is primarily used by individuals to manage their own digital images, and the majority of the tags are users tagging photos they created themselves. This is not absolute; the system has the option of allowing users designated as friends or family to tag users' photos. Additionally, users can enter images created by others into the system, often from web sites. This use of the system is much more like Delicious.

Both Delicious and Flickr are used by individuals to organize materials with their own vocabulary of terms. Individuals have an incentive to tag their materials with terms that will help them organize their collections in a way that they can find these items later. The organizational scheme that emerges for each individual reflects their individual information needs. Conversely, both Delicious and Flickr are services designed to share materials. The individual organizational behavior takes place in a public virtual space on these web sites. Therefore the behavior of the users can also be thought of as being influenced and related to their relationship to the other individuals using the service, and specific groups of users who they share tag use with. It is perhaps harder to justify this model simply from examination of the tags used, but there is definitely evidence of communication and perhaps even community formation through metadata, which will be discussed later.

AREAS FOR FURTHER RESEARCH

Quantitative Tag Analysis : Investigation of the quantitative aspects of tags is an area that could yield some interesting data on the formation and use of the keywords used to describe objects. Another area is to examine the distribution of tag use. Quantitative research in this area will give a better indication of whether a folksonomy converges on terms and foster consensus, or the vocabulary grows as the user-based system grows.

Qualitative User Analysis : The quantitative study of tagging behaviour of the users belonging to different socio-economic and socio-cultural groups is a vital aspect. The main point is to become aware of the users' behaviour in assigning tags to different objects.

Applicability to other systems : Delicious and Flickr are large web services designed to organize and share digital works. The applicability of user generated free-tagging as an organizational construct in other contexts needs further investigation. The systems with an existing social network may be possible area for such study. The use of a folksonomy to supplement existing classification schemes and provide additional access to materials by encouraging and leveraging explicit user metadata contributions is another possible area for research and further development in information retrieval systems.

CONCLUSION

A folksonomic approach in information space holds simultaneously some plus and minus points. Its uncontrolled nature is fundamentally chaotic, suffers from problems of imprecision and ambiguity. Probably this chaos and turmoil will be cleared after an effective re-modeling by the organized systems of controlled vocabularies. Conversely, systems employing free-form tagging that are encouraging users to organize information in their own ways are supremely responsive to user needs and vocabularies, and involve the users of information actively in the organizational system. Overall, transforming the creation of explicit metadata for resources from an isolated, professional activity into a shared, communicative activity by users is an important development that should be explored and considered for future systems development.

Michael Zhang suggested 7 tips for assigning a tag in the following URL and given below: (http://www.folksonomy.org/2006/10/7_tips_for_naming_your_startup/)

1. Keep Length at a Minimum

What's easier to type in multiple a times for day for a simple web search, *Google.com* or *AskJeeves.com*? It's clear why *AskJeeves* shortened their name to *Ask*. If you can't beat competition on quality and functionality, you'd better be aiming to make it as easy as possible for users to access your service. How easily a domain name is typed can make a big difference in whether or not a visitor will want to visit often. Part of the reason I read *CNN.com* for news is how easily the three letters can be typed into the address bar. A good length for one word names is five to six letters. Names should typically also never exceed two words.

2. Be Generic or Be Original

When *Flickr* exploded in popularity, quite a few entrepreneurs seemed to think that it set some sort of de facto standard for Web 2.0 naming conventions. It didn't. Naming your service Locatr, Bookmarkr, Zooomr, Preloadr, or Frappr doesn't put you next in line on the *Yahoo* acquisition queue. Either go for an expensive generic name that accurately describes what you're about, or be creative by choosing an effective and unique name that stands out.

3. Encourage Word of Mouth

Company names should not be difficult to pronounce or spell. If a name doesn't roll of the tongue, then choose something simpler. Can you imagine people around the world asking each other, "Have you heard of the web service PriceWaterhouseCoopers?" Well, neither can I. Once a name has gone from one person's mouth to another person's ear, there shouldn't be any confusion as to how its spelled when typed into a browser.

4. Capture the .com

When Nintendo revealed that their seventh-generation console would be named "Wii", the domain name *Wii.com* was already registered by someone else. Luckily for them, they had the money it took to acquire the domain from the existing owner. If your pockets aren't as deep as Nintendo's, think about working your name around to fit a .com instead of working domain extensions around to fit your name. Even if a domain is unavailable, look up the whois information on the domain and attempt to negotiate for it directly from the existing owner. Ever wonder how many extra hits Disney's *dig.com* gets because of the popularity of *Digg*? It would greatly benefit Digg if they got their hands on Dig.com, but I doubt Disney would sell now. This is also why *thefacebook.com* quickly purchased *facebook.com* from the existing owner when they had the money to do so.

5. Avoid Using Hyphens

Only in special circumstances do hyphens benefit a website (e.g. *experts-exchange.com* instead of *expertsexchange.com*), but in most cases they don't. Don't burden your startup with a hyphen in the domain name just because the hyphen-less domain was already registered. How do you tell some to go to a website if there's a hyphen in the name? If *Myspace* used the domain name my-space.com, how many people a day would erroneously type in myspace.com? There's a whole industry of people who specialize in profiting off typo domains. Don't feed them with your ignorance.

6. Avoid Domain Hacks

Yes, there was a time when it was creative and unique to name your service something like *Del.icio.us*, but now domain hacks have gone from being special to being inconvenient. That's probably why Yahoo acquired the domain name *delicious.com* as an alternative (and easier) way to access the service through the address bar. Words in the English language don't usually have multiple periods within them, therefore it takes more brainpower and time to type them in (both of which are a limited resource these days). If for some reason you just have to use a domain hack, register the .com version and forward it to your domain hack, like *competitious.com.*

7. Keep it Meaningful

We all know generic domain names are hard to come by these days. That, however, does not mean it's hard to come up with a quality name for your company. An easy trick to an effective name is to combine a descriptive word with a meaningful, generic word. Examples include Feed/Burner, You/Tube, Hot/Mail, Tech/Crunch, etc... Make sure the descriptive word gives people a clear idea of what exactly your company does. The meaningful word should make sense and suggest something positive. Naming your startup something like FeedPorcupine or PictureSloth wouldn't fit this rule. Don't do it.

11
Domain Ontology

The term "Ontology" was originated in philosophy. An ontology is an explicit specification of a conceptualization. Ontological categories define the concepts that exist in the domain, as well as relationships between these concepts. According to Guarino et al. (1995), "*Ontology*" can be understood as an intentional semantic structure which encodes the implicit rules constraining the structure of a piece of reality. A domain ontology is a particular type of ontology, which is focused on a specific aspect or facet on the universe of knowledge. Ontologies are thus aimed at answering the question "What kinds of objects exist in one or another domain of the real world and how are they interrelated?" An ontology thus describes the logical structure of a domain, its concepts and the relations between them. Taxonomy implies hierarchy in tree format, while ontology is a web of relationships in graphical layout. The graphs on web can represent any relationship topology. Knowledge acquisition and processing about one or another problem domain is based on ontologies. The ontology of a problem domain thus specifies concepts and relations about which knowledge is to be accumulated and processed. In computer and information science ontology represents a cluster of inter-related concepts along with the relational aspects in details. In the process of classification of the universe of knowledge (As the case was in Dewey Decimal Classification or Library of Congress Classification), one particular subject was delved more to probe into detail, while the inter-relationships among concepts were generally overlooked. But the speciality of domain ontology is that, here the mutual and also self relationships among the concepts and also within a concept are focused. Domain Ontology defines a domain and also indicates the properties of a domain. The term "Domain" points out a very specific area under a broad discipline. For object-oriented applications, domain ontology defines the meta-model for application models in this domain. Ontological categories correspond to the meta-classes for application objects. For example, the economic agent specified by the REA-ontology is a meta-class for objects such as customer and vendor. Economic event is a meta-class for objects such as sale and payment receipt. Economic resource is a meta-class for objects such as money and item. Likewise, relationships between ontological categories become meta-relationships for the relationships between application object, such as stock-flow is a meta-relationship for relationships called outflow and inflow. Traditional general classification schemes provided a macroscopic approach to the universe of knowledge, while domain ontology has a domain-specific approach on the entire knowledge spectrum, which is a microscopic approach. Domain Ontologies are used in artificial intelligence, the Semantic Web, software engineering, biomedical informatics, library science and information architecture as a form of knowledge representation.

The term "Domain" indicates a narrow specific subject space. The texts within a domain generally include three types of words:

1) General-lexicon or dictionary words appearing in

any text. Such words include articles, prepositions, or the words like have, give, see, number, etc. Any information on such words can be easily found in existing dictionaries.

2) Technical terms used in a wider area of knowledge, such as program, software etc.

3) Terms specific for the selected domain, such as cytokinesis, M-phase etc. in the Biological process domain. In domain ontology we are only interested in the latter type of words, i.e. domain-specific terms. These terms have some special properties as compared with the general words or broad-domain terms as given below:

    1) They are not homonymous (polysemous), i.e., they are unambiguous. In any text dealing with some general-topic, the word "Cell division" can refer to partition of a room or segmentation of any department. But in the chosen narrow domain of Biological process, it only can mean a cellular physiological process.

    2) They usually are not synonymous. In general topic text "M-phase" can be substituted with a state of any phenomena, but in the chosen domain it means only a state in the Meiotic cell cycle.

As a domain ontology is a cluster of inter-related concepts represented by words within a chosen domain, the relationships can form different patterns, i.e. either genus-species relationship, or part-whole relationship, or associative relationship. The relationship among the words may either be subordination, or co-ordination, or super-ordination in a given domain. Domain ontology apprehends better understanding and optimum usage of information. It increases the access and sharing of information. It encounters concepts specific to a domain, for instance, Fermi liquid, Luttinger liquid, Kondo effect,

Hubbard model etc. These keywords belong to the domain of condensed matter physics. A top-level ontology or global ontology, on the other hand, includes general concepts independent of a specific domain (e.g. space, time etc.). An Application Ontology, however comprises the concepts that are specialised in a particular context and use, e.g. Fixer, Developer, Exposure time etc. These keywords are related with photo development. Domain ontology is derived from global or top-level ontology, as domains are created from a broad area of discipline. A domain consists of so many specific areas, and some areas gradually achieve practical relevance. The ontology developed on practically relevant areas is known as Application ontology.

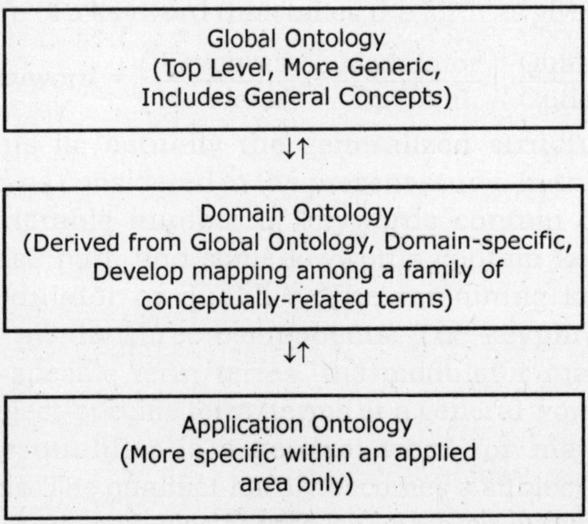

Fig. 11.1

The features contained in an ontology spectrum are shown here. At the low end of expressiveness is a 'Taxonomy,' which is a hierarchy of terms, with each being a sub-class of a more general term. The consecutive levels are Thesaurus, Conceptual Model and Logical Theory respectively.

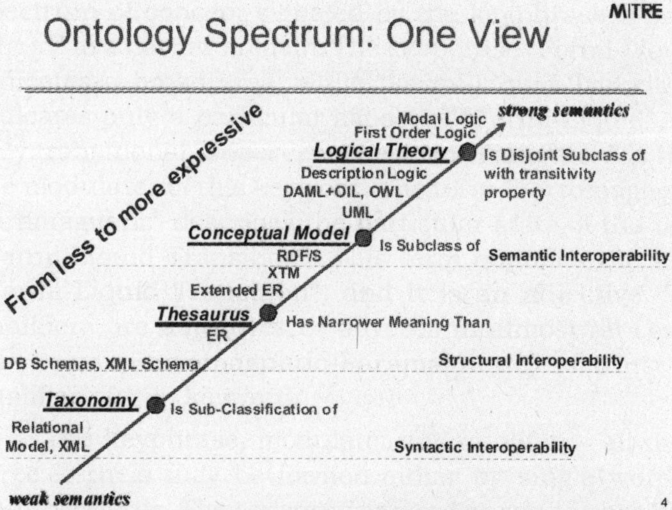

Fig. 11.2 : Ontology Spectrum by Dr. Leo Obrst (*Source* : http://colab.cim3.net/file/work/SICoP/2007-08-09/JSchoening03272007.doc)

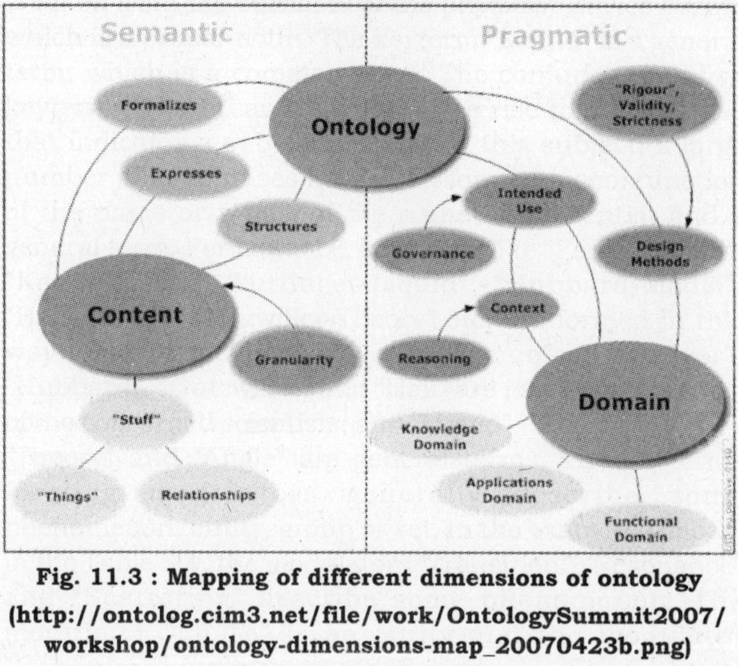

Fig. 11.3 : Mapping of different dimensions of ontology (http://ontolog.cim3.net/file/work/OntologySummit2007/workshop/ontology-dimensions-map_20070423b.png)

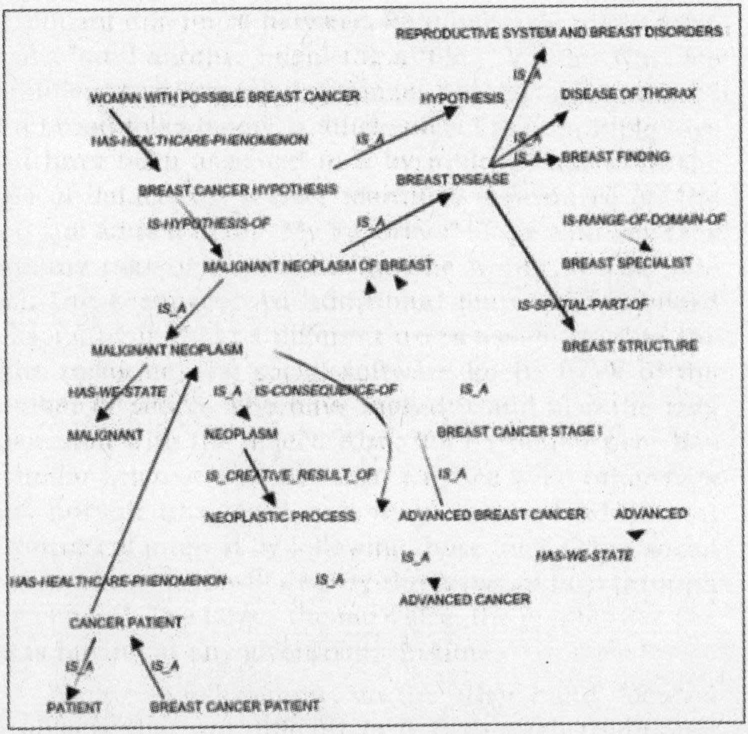

Fig. 11.4: Domain Ontology of cancerous diseases (www.ontologyonline.org)

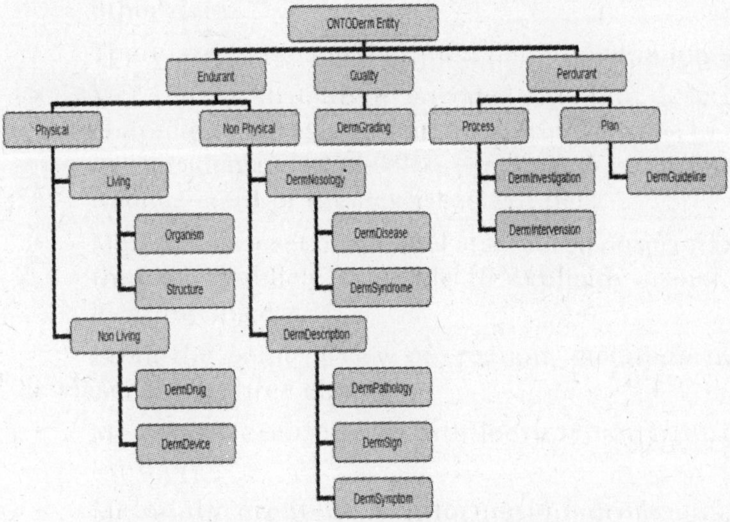

Fig. 11.5: Domain Ontology of Dermatology (http://dermatology.cdlib.org/146/commentary/onto_derm/2.jpg)

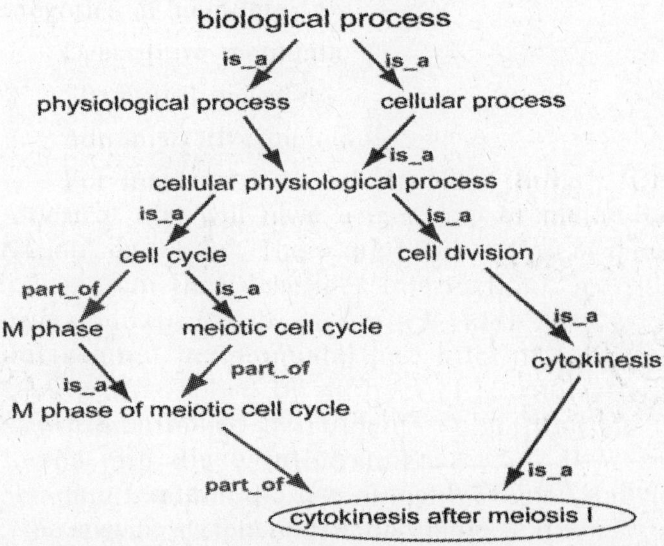

Fig. 11.6: Domain Ontology of Biological Process (http://www.yeastgenome.org/help/images/cytokinesisDAGrels.jpg)

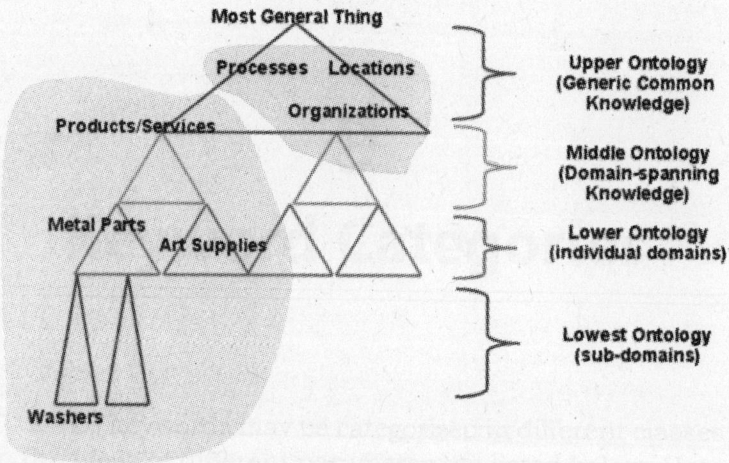

Fig. 11.7: Four levels of ontology (http://ontologyonline.org/visualisation/c/Directory/Air_traffic_services_ontology)

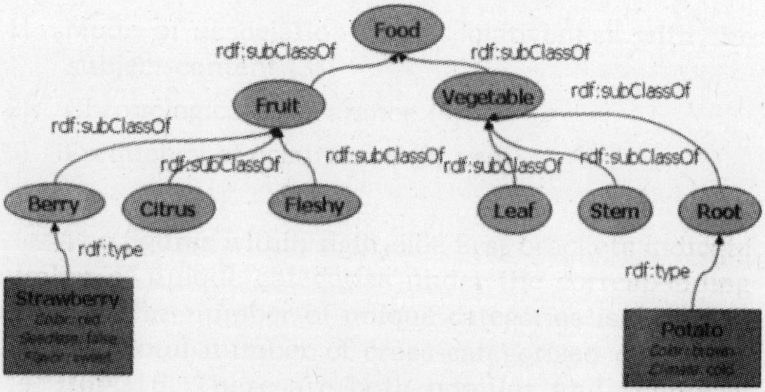

Fig. 11.8: Domain Ontology of Food (www.ontologyonline.org)

12

Semantic Web Concept

According to Wikipedia, The Semantic Web is an evolving extension of the World Wide Web in which the semantics of information and services on the web is defined, making it possible for the web to understand and satisfy the requests of people and machines to use the web content. It derives from World Wide Web Consortium director Sir Tim Berners-Lee's vision of the Web as a universal medium for data, information, and knowledge exchange.

At its core, the semantic web comprises a set of design principles, collaborative working groups, and a variety of enabling technologies. Some elements of the semantic web are expressed as prospective future possibilities that are yet to be implemented or realized. Other elements of the semantic web are expressed in formal specifications. Some of these include Resource Description Framework (RDF), a variety of data interchange formats (e.g. RDF/XML, N3, Turtle, N-Triples), and notations such as RDF Schema (RDFS) and the Web Ontology Language (OWL), all of which are intended to provide a formal description of concepts, terms, and relationships within a given knowledge domain.

The term Web 3.0 is synonymously used for "Semantic web". According to Wikipedia, "Web 3.0" is one of the terms used to describe the evolutionary stage of the Web that follows Web 2.0. Given that technical and social possibilities identified in this latter term are yet to be fully realized the nature of defining Web 3.0 is highly speculative. In general it refers to aspects of the internet which, though potentially possible, are not technically or practically feasible at this time.

The phrase "Web 3.0" was coined by John Markoff of the New York Times in 2006. He referred to a third generation of Internet-based services that collectively comprise what might be called 'the intelligent Web'. The tools that will construct necessary framework for "Web 3.0" are: semantic web, microformats, natural language search, data mining, machine learning, recommendation agents, artificial intelligence technologies etc. This extended web-enabled environment will emphasize on more productive and intuitive user experience.

Nova Spivack defines Web 3.0 as the third decade of the Web (2010–2020) during which he suggests several major complementary technology trends will reach new levels of maturity simultaneously including the following components:

- Transformation of the Web from a network of separately soloed applications and content repositories to a more seamless and interoperable whole.
- Ubiquitous connectivity, broadband adoption, mobile Internet access and mobile devices;
- Network computing, software-as-a-service business models, Web services interoperability, distributed computing, grid computing and cloud computing;
- Open technologies, open APIs and protocols, open data formats, open-source software platforms and open data (e.g. Creative Commons, Open Data License);

- Open identity, OpenID, open reputation, roaming portable identity and personal data;
- The intelligent web, Semantic Web technologies such as RDF, OWL, SWRL, SPARQL, GRDDL, semantic application platforms, and statement-based data-stores;
- Distributed databases, the "World Wide Database" (enabled by Semantic Web technologies); and
- Intelligent applications, natural language processing, machine learning, machine reasoning, autonomous agents.

In an article entitled "Does the Semantic Web = Web 3.0?", Nova Spivack expressed the following views:

(http://novaspivack.typepad.com/nova_spivacks_weblog/2006/11/does_the_semant.html)

"John Markoff's New York Times article discusses the term "Web 3.0" and equates it with the next evolution of the Web, in which he predicts a move towards more intelligent applications.

First of all I want to say that I hope the use of the term "Web 3.0" in the article doesn't distract from the real story here. Because there is actually a story — the Web is gradually evolving into a more intelligent medium. One of the key enabling technologies that will make this possible is the emerging Semantic Web.

I agree with Markoff that the Web is moving towards a new era of more intelligent apps. I also think that this intelligence will be enabled by adding more semantics to the data. But does this evolution qualify for a new name like Web 3.0? For that matter, what does the term Web 2.0 refer to, while we're on the subject?

If you believe that the term Web 2.0 refers to something distinct from the Web we already had before that term was originated, then yes, the Semantic Web is Web 3.0. But from another perspective, Web 2.0, Web

3.0 or Web 12.0 will not be separate from the Web we already have (Web 1.0) — it's all just one big Web. All this technology is connected to the same network.

I think Web 2.0 has taken on a certain meaning over time — focused around application interoperability on the Web using mashups, APIs and widgets, and perhaps also social features like tagging. But I remember when the term Web 2.0 first came out — people thought it was unnecessary and railed against it in fact. Today it has become an industry standard term. So you never know, maybe the term Web 3.0 will catch on.

Web 3.0 is about making all this technology and content smarter — by adding semantics to the data (using the Semantic Web and microformats, etc.) and by adding more smarts to applications so that they can do a better job of helping humans (natural language search, semantic search, recommendation agents, etc.).

So while we probably don't need another label — I would at least say that "Web 3.0" is less intimidating than the term "Semantic Web" to many. On the other hand, I can see a potential confusion arising from terms like Web X.0 as well.

Regardless of what we call it however, I'm just interested in bringing more semantics to the Web. This is a long-effort — it's a marathon not a sprint — and it is already happening, and will continue to happen. It's a technological evolution that must happen in fact. Because the only other alternative to making the Web smarter would be to have computers that are a million times faster than those we have today. Rather than waiting for that to happen, we can just add a little more semantics to today's data and applications to get big benefits. Those of us working with RDF and the Semantic Web have seen the proof of this. In time, so will broader sets of users and developers."

Like the web, the semantic web is not an application;

it is an infrastructure on which many different applications (like electronic commerce) will develop. The usage does not precede the technology, but it explodes when the technology is available. There seem to be two approaches to the application of the semantic web:

1) Semantic web applications for the organizations such as the development of ontology-based market places for business to business electronic commerce or the bioinformatics knowledge grid in which biological data and knowledge bases are seamlessly interconnected and computing resources are available.
2) Semantic web applications for the masses such as intelligent personal assistant gathering and filtering relevant information and composing it in a coherent picture with regard to the user preferences.

More generally, knowledge management, personal or corporate, can take advantage of the semantic web. The semantic web will provide value to any semantically annotated resource by facilitating its retrieving when appropriate.

The objective of the semantic web is to provide a better help to people who take the advantage of the content of the Web. The information on the web should thus be expressed in a logical sequence accessible to computers. The semantic web develops necessary framework for supplying the web with formalized knowledge in addition to its actual informal content. Such formalization ranges from metadata schemes (like the Dublin core metadata markers) to full-fledged logical representation languages. This exists only for particular applications (e.g. SHOE, Ontobroker) and is currently limited to a small part of the web. Now, Googling is an essential function in our daily life. Seeking of any bit ends in Google. But what we are getting there actually? We get millions of responses to a single query and we are forced to scan through many pages to find what we are exactly looking for. We need new search engine to be based on logically related strings amid various concepts. The onward march towards next generation of web search engine technology already geared up. One such example is SHOE that uses XML-like tags and advanced artificial intelligence technology to make keyword based search engines a thing of the past. This is a next generation web search engine. It chalks out seven steps to issue a query: (http://www.cs.umd.edu/projects/plus/SHOE/search/)

1. Select an ontology. The pull-down list allows you to select from one of the available ontologies. By default, the base ontology is selected for you.
2. Select the category that best describes the subject of your query. The list displays all terms used by the ontology. Subcategories are indented beneath their parent categories.
3. Press the Select button. A list of properties that apply to the category you have chosen is displayed to the right of the category list.
4. Enter your query terms. Type in values (e.g., URLs, names, numbers, etc.) for those properties which you wish to use to restrict your search. Use the Show checkbox to display a property in your query results without restricting it to a particular value. Use the Find button to display all instances that have a value for that property and the corresponding values. To use one of these values in your query, select it and press the Add To Query button.
5. Press the Query button. The results of your query are displayed below the category list and properties. Click and drag on the borders between column headings to change the size of columns.
6. View a Web page. Double-click on a URL or select one and press Get Page to open another window

that displays the web page.

7. Issue the same query to the general web. Press Web Search to issue a similar query to a popular search engine.

The basic idea is that all pages indexed by the search engine must use a special set of tags. Say, for example, sort of meta-tags on Fermi liquid. These tags provide more than keywords and descriptions, they describe content and relationships. However, XML alone cannot solve the search problem. Because there is no machine understandable meaning associated with ordinary XML tags, for example a furniture store might use the tag <CHAIR> to mean something you sit on while a university might use the same tag to mean a person that heads a department. As a result, traditional search engines will be just as confused with XML as they are now with HTML. The SHOE solution, however, solves this problem by associating a context with a web page; this context can be used to disambiguate terms and provide background knowledge that might help in interpreting content. SHOE, the new generation search engine uses an ontology with a vocabulary.

The OntoBroker is another most comprehensive and fastest, highly scalable Semantic Web-Middleware. Ontobroker exploits semantic structures by evaluating axioms about concepts, objects, relations between objects and attributes of objects. It is the only commercial inference machine for the processing of ontologies, which supports all W3C recommended Semantic Web languages: OWL (Web Ontology Language), RDF (Resource Description Framework), SPARQL (Query Language for RDF) and, in addition, the industry standard F-Logic. One of the challenges of the current semantic web developments is the design of a framework in which all these understanding can collaborate, because the full benefit of the semantic web can only be attained when computers relate resources from various sources.

The key requirement for the semantic web is interoperability. If machines have to take advantage of web resources, they must be able to access them and use them. As a consequence, the resources must be open and understandable. The resources should not be hidden in a proprietary system which only publishes information in a human or tool-oriented format; on the contrary, they must be invokable and should be published in an open, structured and rich format that let the machines make the best out of them. The semantic web is not just a search engine. It is not only a knowledge representation or natural language processing or language (XML, RDF, DAML+OIL, etc.). It is to be developed on several layers as presented in figure 11.1. An infrastructure will allow identifying, locating, and transforming resources in a robust and safe way. Languages are necessary for expressing the content of the semantic web; the semantics of these languages is sanctioned by inferences engines. Resources such as ontologies, transformations, metadata, and databases must feed these two base layers. The resources of the semantic web are exploited by applications that run on devices.

Client devices
↓
Applications
↓
Resources
↓
Languages
↓
Infrastructure

Fig. 12.1: Layered view of the semantic web

The development of the semantic web will involve efforts in many areas of computer science, i.e. web technology, knowledge representation, database, automated theorem proving, knowledge engineering, computer-supported cooperative work, human-computer interaction, natural language processing, etc. Moreover, the semantic web must not be separated from many aspects, i.e. personalization (and thus privacy issues), mobility (and thus reliability issues), publication (and thus security issue). These issues are quite traditional but the semantic web drives them to their extreme because the use of semantically grounded languages makes the computer actions more powerful and the threats more acute. The semantic web is not just a matter of technology, economics, and social matters. All these aspects must be articulated in an integrated and logical way to provide real value to its users.

LIST OF WEBSITES ON SEMANTIC WEB

Annotea Project

Live early adoption and demonstration project enhancing the W3C collaboration environment with shared annotations.

Big Fractal Tangle

Daily reflections on the ongoing evolution of the Semantic Web.

The Cognitive Web

A human-centric web architecture comprised of semantic markup and fuzzy logics.

Conceptual Graphs and SWeb

Comparison of Conceptual Graphs as a logic layer to RDF.

cwm

A general purpose data processor written in Python.

Core language is RDF, extended to include rules, using RDF/XML or RDF/N3 serializations as required.

EpiSem Action

European research project with the goal to develop a software framework for building ontology-based collaboration platforms.

Euler Proof Mechanism

A backward-chaining reasoner based on RDF and OWL, using resolution inference mechanism and following Euler paths.

The Future of the Semantic Web

Article on the semantic web and its significance for the scientific community by Dr. Albert Benschop (University of Amsterdam).

Gnowsis

A framework for a personal semantic desktop system.

HP Labs Semantic Web Research

Works to further the vision through research, development and internal promotion. Features technology, tools, resources and contact information.

ICS-FORTH RDFSuite: High-level Scalable Tools for the Semantic Web

Tools for managing voluminous RDF description bases.

ILRT Semantic Web Research Group

Tools for storage and query of structured data and applications for digital libraries and project management. From the Institute for Learning and Research Technology at the University of Bristol.

Inference Web

Framework for explaining Semantic Web tasks by storing, exchanging, combining, annotating, comparing and rendering proofs fragments provided by engines embedded in Semantic Web applications.

INTAP Semantic Web Committee

Committee in Japan to produce research and development in the Semantic Web.

IsaViz Overview

A visual authoring tool for RDF.

Jeff Heflin's Publications

Provide abstracts of downloadable technical papers on various Semantic Web topics like Dynamic Ontologies and Semantic Interoperability.

KAON Ontology and Semantic Web Infrastructure

Open source ontology management infrastructure. Includes a tool suite allowing easy ontology creation and management, as well as building ontology-based applications.

2nd International Semantic Web Conference (ISWC2003)

Upcoming meeting with calls for papers, sponsors, workshop and tutorial proposals, demos, and posters.

Next Web Generation

A Research Group from University of Innsbruck involved in various projects combining and improving recent trends like Web Services, Semantic Portals and Grid Technology.

OntoWare

Collaborative project management and development environment for the Semantic Web

OpenSHORE.org

Semantic Hypertext Object Repository. A repository with a free definable meta model where structured documents can be imported after parsing and transforming into XML.

Personal Data Protection in the Semantic Web

Masters of Engineering Thesis with a focus on PEDAL: Personal Data Access Language.

Platypus Wiki

Uses RDF, RDF Schema, and OWL to create ontologies and manage metadata.

Practical Knowledge Representation for the Web

Survey and analysis of traditional, new, and arising Web standards and how they can be used to represent machine-processable semantics of Web sources.

Retsina Semantic Web Calendar Agent

Project to develop interoperability between RDF based calendar descriptions and Personal Information Manager Systems such as Microsoft's Outlook.

SEKT Project

European project on developing Semantically Enabled Knowledge Technologies.

Semantic Patterns Language

Explores Universal Semantic Code to help create applications for Semantic WEB.

The Semantic Web

Lengthy descriptive Scientific American article by Tim Berners-Lee, James Hendler and Ora Lassila. (May, 2001)

The Semantic Web: 1-2-3

An XML hacker discusses XML, RDF and the Semantic Web. Features links to other resources.

Semantic Web In One Day

Experiment in applying and assembling existing Semantic Web technologies in one day.

Semantic Web Research Group

People from the Maryland Information and Network Dynamics Lab working on the Semantic Web.

Semantic Weblog

A weblog about PhD research on Semantic Web services and multiagent systems.

SemDis - Discovering Complex Relationships in Semantic Web

A research project focused on design, prototyping and evaluation of a system that supports indexing and querying complex semantic relationships from the Web.

The SEWASIE project: Semantic Webs and AgentS in Integrated Economies

SEWASIE is a collaboration of a number of research groups aiming to design and implement an advanced search engine accessing heterogeneous data sources on the web, using semantic enrichment to provide the basis of structured secure web-based communication.

SWAD-Europe Thesaurus Activity

Open source systems and guidelines for using thesauri in a semantic web environment.

TOOL: The Open Opinion Layer

Paper exploring the development of a distributed open opinion architecture.

TopQuadrant

Company that providing consulting and tools for architectural design and implementation of Semantic Technology Solutions with an emphasis on Ontology Engineering.

URI Query Agent Model

URIQA proposes an extension to web architecture used to indicate to a web server that it should resolve the specified URI in terms of knowledge about the resource denoted by that URI rather than in terms of a representation of the resource.

W3C Semantic Web Activity Statement

The W3C Semantic Web Activity has been established to serve a leadership role, in both the design of specifications and the open, collaborative development of technology for the Semantic Web.

Weaving the Web

The original design and ultimate destiny of the World Wide Web, by its inventor, Tim Berners-Lee. Features a linked glossary, a time line, errata and an excerpt from Chapter 1.

Semantic Web Applications and Perspectives

The first Italian Workshop on Semantic Web Applications and Perspectives in collaboration with the W3C Italian Office. (December 10, 2004)

The Next Web

Article discusses the changes expected in the Web's next evolution. Written by David M. Ewalt; published in "Information Week." (October 14, 2002)

The Semantic Web Lifts Off

Article on W3C's Semantic Web activity. (October 1, 2002)

The Languages of the Semantic Web

Article by Uche Ogbuji discusses the limits of today's Web and the challenge of how agents can infer relationships and act on them. Originally published in the "New Architect" e-zine. (June 1, 2002)

The Semantic Web: It's Whom You Know

Discusses the problems with current notions, popularity ranking and collaborative filtering and suggests next steps. By Andy Oram, published in O'Reilly Network. (April 19, 2002)

Building a Semantic Web Site

Even though the Semantic Web may yet seem a remote dream, there are already tools one can use to make a tiny step forward by building "semantic web sites," which can be much easier to navigate than ordinary sites. (May 2, 2001)

The Semantic Web

Lengthy descriptive Scientific American article by Tim Berners-Lee, James Hendler and Ora Lassila. (May, 2001)

The Semantic Web: A Primer

Offers an introduction and discusses technologies and developments. By Edd Dumbill, published in O'Reilly XML.com. (November 1, 2000)

Semantic Web Roadmap

An attempt to give a high-level plan of the architecture by Tim Berners-Lee. (September 14, 1998)

13

Web 2.0 and Library 2.0

(*"Web 2.0 is an attitude not a technology",*
Ian Davies, 2005)

(*"Web 2.0 is based on wisdom of crowds",*
Stephen Abram, 2007)

According to Wikipedia, "Web 2.0 describes the changing trends in the use of World Wide Web technology and web design that aim to enhance creativity, secure information sharing, collaboration and functionality of the web. Web 2.0 concepts have led to the development and evolution of web-based communities and hosted services, such as social-networking sites, video sharing sites, wikis, blogs, and folksonomies. The term became notable after the first O'Reilly Media Web 2.0 conference in 2004. Although the term suggests a new version of the World Wide Web, it does not refer to an update to any technical specifications, but rather to changes in the ways software developers and end-users utilize the Web". According to Tim O'Reilly, "Web 2.0 is the business revolution in the computer industry caused by the move to the Internet as a platform, and an attempt to understand the rules for success on that new platform".

There is very limited scope of user interaction and

participation in World Wide Web (www). As reported by Tim O'Reilly (http://radar.oreilly.com/archives/2005/09/what-is-web-20.html), the leader of Web 2.0 concept, the concept of "Web 2.0" began with a conference brainstorming session on interactive user-driven web, organized by O'Reilly and MediaLive International in 2005. Just within a year, web 2.0 became a catchword with more than citations in Google. The concept of web 2.0 was shaped from the process of measuring the reasons for success of some Internet companies in comparison with their competitors. The heart of the concept of web 2.0 is the networking. Tim O'Reilly posted a more compact definition of web 2.0 in blogosphere, i.e. "Web 2.0 is the network as platform, spanning all connected devices. Web 2.0 applications are those that make the most of the intrinsic advantages of that platform: delivering software as a continually-updated service that gets better the more people use it, consuming and remixing data from multiple sources, including individual users, while providing their own data and services in a form that allows remixing by others, creating network effects through an "architecture of participation," and going beyond the page metaphor of Web 1.0 to deliver rich user experiences".

An analysis of this definition reveals the following key characteristics of Web 2.0:

- Web-based applications can be accessed from anywhere
- Simple applications solve specific problems
- Data can be readily shared
- Distribution is bottom-up, not top-down
- Employees and customers can access and use tools on their own
- Social tools encourage people to create, collaborate, edit, categorize, exchange, and promote information
- Network effects are encouraged; the more people who contribute, the better the content gets

In Web 1.0, a small number of writers created Web pages for a large number of readers. As a result, people could get information by going directly to the source: Adobe.com for graphic design issues, Microsoft.com for Windows issues, and CNN.com for news. Over time more and more people started writing content in addition to reading it. As a result, suddenly there was too much information to keep up with. As time is limited for everyone, it is impossible to visit each and every site for almost everybody. In the knowledge society, information is considered as a strategic resource in its own right and a major fraction of people in the society are involved in information organisation and dissemination. The volume of the published material also started to gallop with the increase in number of information disseminators. In such situation, it became apparent that the Web 1.0 paradigm had to change.

In Web 2.0 culture, a vision of the Web in which information is broken up into "microcontent" units, can be distributed over dozens of domains. The Web of documents has morphed into a Web of data. People are no longer just looking to the same old sources for information. Now we're looking to a new set of tools to aggregate and remix microcontent in new and useful ways. These tools, the interfaces of Web 2.0, will become the frontier of design innovation. Ian Davies remarked, "Web 1.0 took people to information, Web 2.0 will take information to the people." This is the core sense of web 2.0 culture. Let us present 25 basic contrasting features between web 1.0 and web 2.0 below. Some features were collected from (http://www.darrenbarefoot.com/archives/2006/05/web-10-vs-web-20.html). This will make clear the essential amendments and step-ups of web 2.0 in comparison with web 1.0.

1. Web 1.0 was about reading, Web 2.0 is about writing.

2. Web 1.0 was about companies, Web 2.0 is about communities.
3. Web 1.0 was about client-server, Web 2.0 is about peer to peer.
4. Web 1.0 was about HTML, Web 2.0 is about XML.
5. Web 1.0 was about home pages, Web 2.0 is about blogs.
6. Web 1.0 was about lectures, Web 2.0 is about conversation.
7. Web 1.0 was about advertising, Web 2.0 is about word of mouth.
8. Web 1.0 was about services sold over the web, Web 2.0 is about web services.
9. Web 1.0 was top-down. Web 2.0 is bottom-up.
10. Web 1.0 contained directories, Web 2.0 encounters tagging.
11. Web 1.0 was based on taxonomy, Web 2.0 is based on folksonomy.
12. Web 1.0 focused on personal web sites, Web 2.0 focused on blogging.
13. Web 1.0 focused on Britannica Online, Web 2.0 focuses on Wikipedia.
14. Web 1.0 focused on Mp3.com, Web 2.0 focuses on Napster.
15. Web 1.0 focused on publishing, Web 2.0 focuses on participation.
16. Web 1.0 focused on Ofoto, Web 2.0 focuses on Flickr.
17. Web 1.0 was edited and produced. Web 2.0 is raw.
18. Web 1.0 was banner ads. Web 2.0 is Adsense.
19. Web 1.0 was text. Web 2.0 is video.
20. Web 1.0 was professional. Web 2.0 is amateur.
21. Web 1.0 was dial up. Web 2.0 is broadband.
22. Web 1.0 was IE. Web 2.0 is FireFox.

23. Web 1.0 was information. Web 2.0 is opinion.
24. Web 1.0 was a tool. Web 2.0 is a lifestyle.
25. Web 1.0 was a tool for the few. Web 2.0 is entertainment for the many.

Paul Miller enunciated following principles of Web 2.0 (http://www.ariadne.ac.uk/issue45/miller/):

- Web 2.0 presages a freeing of data, allowing it to be exposed, discovered and manipulated in a variety of ways distinct from the purpose of the application originally used to gain access.
- Web 2.0 permits the building of virtual applications, drawing data and functionality from a number of different sources as appropriate.
- Web 2.0 is participative. The traditional Web has tended to be somewhat one-sided, with a flow of content from provider to viewer. Figures from last year suggested that 44% of Internet-using American adults had actively participated online, by blogging, sharing files, or equivalent (http://www.pewinternet.org/pdfs/PIP_Content_Creation_Report.pdf).
- Web 2.0 applications work for the user, and are able to locate and assemble content that meets our needs as users, rather than forcing us to conform to the paths laid out for us by content owners or their intermediaries.
- Web 2.0 applications are modular, with developers and users able to pick and choose from a set of interoperating components in order to build something that meets their needs.
- Web 2.0 is about sharing: code, content, ideas.
- Web 2.0 is about communication and facilitating community. People communicate. The Web facilitated that to a degree, but presented a barrier that hindered the back-and-forth of true communication.

- Web 2.0 is about remix. For too long, we have jumped from one area of the Web to another, struggling with different interfaces, ignoring endless advertisements, and wading through uninteresting content on a site in order to locate the service, document, or snippet that meets our needs. Increasingly, we can unambiguously reference and call upon the service, document or snippet that we require, incorporating it into something new that is both ours and the original contributors'.
- Web 2.0 is smart. Applications will be able to use knowledge of us, where we have been and what we are doing to deliver services that meet our needs.
- Web 2.0 opens up the Long Tail, making it increasingly cost-effective to service the interests of large numbers of relatively small groups of individuals and to enable them to benefit from key pieces of the platform while fulfilling their own needs.
- Web 2.0 is built upon Trust, whether that is trust placed in individuals, in assertions, or in the uses and reuses of data.

Figure 13.1 below shows a "meme map" of Web 2.0 that was developed at a brainstorming session during FOO Camp, a conference at O'Reilly Media. It shows many ideas that radiate out from the Web 2.0 core. Web 2.0 has often been described as "the Web as platform," and if we think about the Web as a platform for interacting with content, we will see how it impacts design. Let us imagine a bunch of content provided by different parties—companies, individuals, governments—upon which interfaces could be built that combine the information in ways no single domain ever could. For example, Amazon.com makes its database of content accessible to the outside world. Anyone can design an interface to replace Amazon's that better suits specific needs, but the power of this is that content can be personalized or remixed with other data to create much more useful tools.

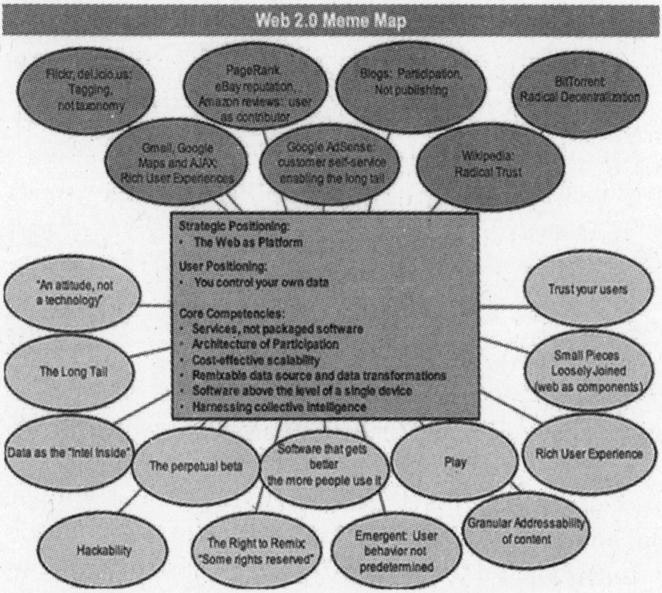

Fig. 13.1. Tim O'Reilly's Web 2.0 'meme map'

Web 2.0 + Library = Library 2.0?

(*"Web 2.0 and libraries are well suited for marriage, and many librarians have recognized so". Jack Maness, 2006)*

Libraries were once the storehouse of knowledge. Traditional library concept encountered just a closed-wall, store-house with stacks of books. The concept of library in knowledge society, however, has undergone through metamorphosis. If a bit of information is exchanged among few people within a network, then that network is well enough to play an active role of library. The concept of invisible college or technological gatekeeper was the predecessor of today's networking platform in web 2.0 environment. Web 2.0 technologies are changing basic ways users interact with information resources and services on web. Since the early days of web, libraries are increasingly using it as a platform to disseminate services. Library and information professionals are closely watching this revolution of web. Various issues related with this transformation are regularly arising on web, particularly in biblioblogosphere. Michael Casey first coined the phrase "Library 2.0" in his blog (www.librarycrunch.com) in 2005. He reported impact of Web 2.0 and possible changes in web-enabled library services. Maness identified essential elements of Library 2.0 and listed Web 2.0 tools that have positive impacts on library services. Some definitions of Library 2.0 are given below to chalk out its core attributes.

- Library 2.0 is a loosely defined model for a modernized form of library service that reflects a transition within the library world in the way that services are delivered to users. The focus is on user-centered change and participation in the creation of content and community. The concept of Library 2.0 borrows from that of Business 2.0 and Web 2.0 and follows some of the same underlying philosophies. This includes online services such as the use of OPAC systems and an increased flow of information from the user back to the library. (Wikipedia)
- It is a model for library service that encourages constant and purposeful changes, inviting user participation in the creation of both the physical and the virtual services they want supported by consistently evaluating services. It also attempt to reach new users and better serve current ones through improved customer-driven offerings. (M.E.Casey and L.C.Savastinuk, January, 2006)
- Library 2.0 is the application of interactive,

collaborative, and multi-media web-based technologies to web-based library services and collections. (Jack Maness, June, 2006)

- Library 2.0 describes a subset of library services designed to meet user needs caused by the direct and peripheral effects of web 2.0. (M.Habib, November, 2006)
- Library 2.0 = (books 'n stuff + people+ radical trust) x participation. (John Blyberg, February, 2007)

With the rise of Google, Amazon, Wikipedia and more, there is an oft-stated fear that many users may bypass traditional institution-based approach for knowledge-seeking that they perceive to be slow, unresponsive and unappealing. Libraries should be seizing every opportunity to challenge these perceptions, and to push their genuinely valuable content, services and expertise out to places where people might stand to benefit from them; places where a user would rarely consider drawing upon a library for support. The definition of library is well-known to everybody. But if we ask one hundred people for a compact definition of Library 2.0, we may get hundred different answers. The precise definition remains open to debate. It is clear that Web 2.0 represents an important shift in the way digital information is created, shared, stored, distributed, and manipulated. Similarly Library 2.0 also represents a significant shift in traditional practices and trends of knowledge and information seeking. This is an essential shift from the traditional approach of isolated study and gathering information to the networked environment of mutual sharing and participation. Web 2.0 describes a set of next-generation Internet technologies. These protocols and tools make it easier to create online applications that behave dynamically, much like traditional PC-based software. They're also highly social, encouraging users to manipulate and interact with content in new ways. Web 2.0 pushes computing power off the desktop and onto the Internet, which means less time and money spent on PC software administration. As a general rule, Web 2.0 tools are also less expensive than traditional software — and many are even free. Because they're Web-based, all we need to get started is an up-to-date browser.

Some Key Facts

Buzz phrase coined: 2004, by Tim O'Reilly of tech publisher O'Reilly Media

Thumbnail definition: Web 2.0 is a set of Web-based software services that encourage users to become more involved in the creation and manipulation of data.

Enabling technologies: AJAX, blogs, RSS, wikis, XML, Atom

Prominent Web 2.0 brands: digg, Flickr, Google Apps, LinkedIn, Salesforce.com, Socialtext, YouTube, Wikipedia

Investment: Web 2.0 startups attracted $844 million in venture capital investment during 2006, more than twice as much as in 2005. (Source: VentureOne)

Strong Impact on Business World

There are some reasons why Web 2.0 is relevant to business people. The first has to do with reducing the costs associated with traditional enterprise applications. For instance, if any software is expensive to install, configure, maintain and upgrade on personal computers and company servers, Web 2.0 tools eliminate much of this hassle and expense because Web 2.0 applications reside on servers maintained by the vendors themselves. Web 2.0 is also changing the way information is created, used, shared, and manipulated. Web 2.0 offers many potential benefits for the business world, but it's a different world indeed.

The Strong Points

Philosophically, Web 2.0 is all about simplicity. Practically, it decouples computing from stand-alone computers — a shift that dramatically reduces software deployment and administrative costs. It uses common software protocols to foster the free exchange of information between different tools and groups of users. As it encourages large-scale collaboration, Web 2.0 facilitates new forms of problem-solving that can provide business managers with valuable ideas and insights.

Key Pioneers in Web 2.0 Theory

Michael Arrington: Just as restaurants, movie producers, and musicians keep an eye on what the critics have to say, so, too, do Web 2.0 startups. (TechCrunch blog).

Mark Benioff: The founder and CEO of Salesforce.com, Benioff was touting the benefits of his company's Web-based customer relationship management (CRM) tools years before the phrase "Web 2.0" was invented.

Tim O'Reilly: The founder of tech publisher O'Reilly Media and a respected industry visionary, O'Reilly helped coin the term "Web 2.0" in 2004 and he's still considered a leading thinker on the subject. O'Reilly's "Most recent definition of Web 2.0" describes it as "the business revolution in the computer industry caused by the move to the Internet as platform, and an attempt to understand the rules for success on that new platform. Chief among those rules is this: Build applications that harness network effects to get better the more people use them."

Venture capitalists: Much of the most interesting activity in Web 2.0 development comes from entrepreneurial startups, and these are usually funded by VC investment. According to VentureOne, in 2006, the most active investors in Web 2.0 startups were

Benchmark Capital, Draper Fisher Jurvetson, Sequoia Capital and Omidyar Network.

Some services and tools that are developing main framework for effective functioning of Library 2.0 are listed below:

AJAX: An acronym derived from "Asynchronous JavaScript and XML." AJAX is an important underlying technology used to create interactive Web applications. Ajax is what enables Web 2.0 sites to behave dynamically, so that they feel more like computer programs than static web pages. Like the way Google Maps lets you drag elements across the page? That's AJAX in action.

Atom: A format for the syndication of online content, atom functions as a newer alternative to RSS (described below).

Blog: Originally derived from the word "weblog," a blog is a simple content website created with inexpensive self-publishing tools. Blogs are the backbone of Web 2.0's democratic spirit.

Del.icio.us: A social bookmarks manager. Using bookmarks, one can append enrich his list to categorize them.

Digg: Interactive news sites where users submit and decide what stories are shown.

Flickr: It is a photo sharing service that allows users to upload, share, comment on and categorize photographs. Users can label photos using tags or keywords, which is effectively subject indexing but without a controlled vocabulary.

Instant Messaging: Allows real-time text communication between individuals.

Jumpcut: Provides free editing tools for uploading, editing and remixing.

LibraryThing: Allows users to catalogue their books and share lists with each other. Librarians can thus interact and recommend their resources to each other. Members can see cover images of the books. They can also review books, form special interest groups and enter DDC number to rearrange books on virtual shelves, and add star rating of books.

Mashups: Websites or applications that combine content from one or more sources. For example, Cellreception.com combines Google Maps with a database of 124,000 cell phone tower locations to help users determine where mobile coverage is strong — and where it isn't.

MySpace and Facebook: Allows users to set up interactive and personalized web profiles with details of personal information.

PaperBackSwap: An interesting Web 2.0 service functioning as a lending library.

Podcasts: A tool for systematic arrangement of audio files, so that the users can download them.

RSS: Shorthand for "Real Simple Syndication," RSS is a protocol that makes it easy for computer users to receive content from their favorite providers whenever the content is updated. Instead of having to remember to visit a website to read a favorite column, watch a video, or listen to an audio program, RSS lets a user subscribe to the content so it's delivered automatically. The flow of content the user receives is called an "RSS feed."

Second Life: It is a subscription based 3D virtual world where registered users interact by building, playing, working and flying alongside other virtual characters. Users can also socialize, connect and create avatars using voice and text chat.

Social media: A generic term used to describe Web-based tools that harness the power of collaboration and group interaction. This can take many forms, from the personal web pages of MySpace to the virtual worlds of Second Life to the professional networking popular on

LinkedIn.

Tags: User-generated keywords used to describe online content. Tags make it easier for both humans and search engines to find relevant and related information.

Technorati: It is a site that provides searching for user-generated media (including weblogs) by tag or keyword. Also provides popularity indexes.

Wikis: A dynamic Web document that allows users to add, change, or edit the content displayed on the page. The user-created Wikipedia online encyclopedia is the most famous example.

Wikimedia: The Wikimedia Foundation, Inc. is a non-profit charitable organization headquartered in San Francisco, California, US, and organized under the laws of the state of Florida, where it was initially based. It operates several online collaborative wiki projects including Wikipedia, Wiktionary, Wikiquote, Wikibooks (including Wikijunior), Wikisource, Wikimedia Commons, Wikispecies, Wikinews, Wikiversity, Wikimedia Incubator and Meta-Wiki. Its flagship project, the English-language Wikipedia, ranks among the top ten most-visited websites worldwide. The main objectives of Wikimedia Foundation are to develop and maintain open content, wiki-based projects and to provide the full contents of those projects to the general public free of charge. In addition to the multilingual general encyclopedia, Wikipedia, the foundation manages a multi-language dictionary and thesaurus named Wiktionary, an encyclopedia of quotations named Wikiquote, a repository of source texts in any language named Wikisource, and a collection of e-book texts for students (such as textbooks and annotated public domain books) named Wikibooks. Wikijunior is a subproject of Wikibooks that consist of books for children. The name "Wikimedia" was coined by Sheldon Rampton. In April 2005, the US Internal Revenue Service approved the Wikimedia foundation as an educational foundation in the category "Adult, Continuing Education" and all contributions to the Wikimedia Foundation are tax deductible at per U.S. income tax regulation.

Wikibooks: Wikibooks is a Wikimedia Foundation project for the creation of free content textbooks and annotated texts that anyone can edit. Wikibooks was launched on July 10, 2003 for a project to host and build free textbooks on subjects such as organic chemistry and physics. Wikibooks is a collection of open-content textbooks, annotated texts, instructional guides and manuals. The materials of Wikibooks can be used in classroom teaching and self-learning as well. Only instructional books are appropriate for inclusion in Wikibooks. The fiction and reference books are not allowed on Wikibooks, unless they are instructional. The materials inappropriate for Wikibooks can be removed in accordance with the deletion policy.

Wikijunior: Wikijunior is a subproject of Wikibooks that specializes in books for children. The project consists of both a magazine and a website, and is currently being developed in English, Danish, Finnish, French, German, Italian, Japanese and Spanish.

WikiMapia: WikiMapia is an online map and satellite imaging resource that combines Google Maps with wiki system, allowing users to add information, in the form of a note, to any location on Earth. It was launched on May 24, 2006 with the aim of describing the whole world. At present, it has almost 9 million places marked.

Wikinews: Wikinews is a free-content news source wiki and a project of the Wikimedia Foundation. In contrast to most projects of the Wikimedia Foundation, Wikinews allows original work under the form of original reporting and interviews.

Wikipedia: Wikipedia is a free, multilingual encyclopedia project supported by the non-profit

Wikimedia Foundation. Its name is derived by coupling two words wiki (a technology for creating collaborative websites) and encyclopedia. Wikipedia's 11 million articles (2.6 million in English) have been written collaboratively by volunteers around the world, and almost all of its articles can be edited by anyone who can access the Wikipedia website. This website was launched in January 2001. It is currently the largest and most popular general reference work on the Internet. Wikipedia is often criticized for its editorial process; lack of reliability and accuracy due to addition of spurious or unverified information. Wikipedia functions not only as an encyclopedic reference but also as a frequently-updated news resource. Wikipedia began as a complementary project for Nupedia, a free online English-language encyclopedia project whose articles were written by experts and reviewed under a formal process. Nupedia was founded on March 9, 2000, under the ownership of Bomis, Inc, a web portal company. The number of English articles in Wikipedia, up to September 9, 2007 was two million. As of November 16, 2008, there are 264 Wikipedia languages, but the portal supports only ten languages.

Wikiquote: Wikiquote is one of a family of wiki-based projects run by the Wikimedia Foundation, running on MediaWiki software. The goal of the project is to produce collaboratively a vast reference of quotations from prominent people, books, films and proverbs, and to give details about them. Like other Wiki projects, in Wikiquote also there are provisions for the visitors to contribute. Wikiquote pages are cross-linked to articles about the notable personalities on Wikipedia. Initially, the project was only in English language, but since July 2004, additional languages were added.

Wikisource: Wikisource is a Wikimedia project to build a free, wiki-library of information, along with translations into any language and other supporting materials. Wikisource collects and stores in digital format previously published texts; including novels, non-fiction works, letters, speeches, constitutional and historical documents, laws and a range of other documents. All texts collected are either free of copyright or released under the GNU Free Documentation License.

Wikispecies: Wikispecies is a wiki-based online project supported by the Wikimedia Foundation. It aims to create a comprehensive free content catalogue of all species. It is aimed at scientists, rather than at the general public. Wikispecies is available under the GNU Free Documentation License. It was started in August 2004, with biologists across the world.

Wikiversity: Wikiversity is a Wikimedia Foundation project, which supports learning communities, their learning materials and resulting activities. It contains a series of course-materials for advancement of learning. Wikiversity is a center for creation and use of free learning materials. It accelerates several learning activities. The primary objectives of Wikiversity are to:

- Create and host a range of free-content, multilingual learning materials/resources, for all age groups in all languages.
- Host scholarly/learning projects and communities that support these materials.

The Wikiversity e-Learning model emphasizes on "learning by doing". Wikiversity's motto is to set learning free. Learning is facilitated through collaboration on projects that are detailed, outlined, summarized or results reported by editing Wikiversity pages. Wikiversity learning projects include collections of wiki webpages concerned with the exploration of a particular topic. Wikiversity participants are encouraged to express their learning goals, and the Wikiversity community collaborates to develop learning activities and projects to accommodate those goals. Wikiversity resources include teaching aids, lesson plans, curricula, links to off-site resources, course notes, example and problem sets, computer simulations, reading lists, and other as devised by participants; but do not include ready-made textbooks. Textbooks are hosted at Wikibooks for update and maintenance. Learning groups in each subject area create a web of resources that form the basis of discussions and activities at Wikiversity.

Wiktionary: Wiktionary is a collaborative project to produce a free-content multilingual dictionary. Wiktionary is the lexical sister of Wikipedia project. It includes a thesaurus, a rhyme guide, phrase books, language statistics and extensive appendices. Only definitions of words are not given here, but the etymologies, pronunciations, sample quotations, synonyms, antonyms and translations are also included.

Writely.com: A free online word processor through which users can create, format, spell check, change fonts and font size and also place images in documents.

XML: An abbreviation for "Extensible Markup Language," XML is a programming code for online data that preserves the structure and formatting of a digital document regardless of whatever application is used to read it. XML is an important enabling technology for RSS feeds.

YouTube: This tool allows users to upload, tag, watch, rate, review, blog and view videos and movie clips.

TOP 100 WEB 2.0 SITES

Top 100 Web 2.0 sites are listed below. The list was collected from Web 2.0 magazine, January 1, 2007 (http://web2magazine.blogspot.com/2007/01/thanks-for-web-2.html).

Programming

1. Ajaxlines : Ajax related tutorials, articles and review, in a web 2.0 design.

2. ma.gnolia : Build your web site and build community online

3. Ajaxian : Ajax related blog

4. Web 2.0 Sites : web 2.0 sites directory, for all web 2.0 related services.

Video

1. YouTube : YouTube is a popular free video sharing Web site which lets users upload, view, and share video clips.

2. Meta Cafe : Metacafe – Get the best internet videos – Funny videos, Amazing clips, Rare movies

3. Vimeo : Share your video clips. Upload video that you shoot with your digital camera, mobile phone, or camcorder. Share video by linking to Vimeo.

4. Daily Motion Publish, tag, organize and share your video clips.

5. Imeem : imeem is a social media service where users interact with each other by watching, posting, and sharing content of all media types, including blogs, photos, audio, and video. In one sense, imeem is a media-centric social network service, and in another sense, it is also a user participation service for online content.

6. ClipShack : ClipShack is a community for videophiles; a destination where people can post their video for general public viewing and comment, share clips with friends and family, post video to blogs, share...

7. vSocial : The fastest, easiest way to upload, watch and share your favorite video clips.

8. Jumpcut : The best place to create, remix and share movies and slideshows online. There's nothing else like it. Jumpcut Makes Movies, Simple.

9. Video Bomb : Video Bomb filters up the hottest videos on the internet: people submit links to the 'Incoming!' page and you bomb the best ones. If a video gets a lot of bombs quickly, it makes it to the front...

10. eyeSpot : Shoot, Mix, and Share your Video. Use the eyespot Mixer to edit and combine your videos, music and photos online! Share your video and mixes with the world for Free

11. revver : Upload, share videos

12. Avidbeauty : Avid Beauty is an entertainment community for iPod users. We offer iPod downloads which are available in playlists known as Podcasts. We also offer Flickr photo, YouTube video and LiveJournal integration into your member profile.

Music

1. last.fm : Generate custom streaming music stations with Last.fm by searching for and tagging your favorite artists. Build your own library and search the libraries of others to find who likes the same music as you

2. Musicovery : Discover new music based on your mood, this free webradio let you browse music styles and epochs

3. read.io : Read.io converts RSS feeds into podcasts via TextToSpeech. Many languages supported.

4. MusicStrands : Search MusicStrands to discover new music. Listen to samples, then tag good tracks and exile the ones you don't like to get clear recommendations, either on site or with an optional iTunes plugin. Then purchase music from a variety of vendors.

5. PODZINGER : PODZINGER – the world's premiere audio and video search engine

6. Upto11 : Using tags and rankings, Upto11 suggests new music for you. Create and share your recommendations, tags, and playlists via a personal user page.

7. Pandora : Pandora is the music discovery service

that helps you find new music based on your old and current favorites

Chat

1. Meebo : meebo, the web messenger that lets you access IM from absolutely anywhere. Meebo supports msn, yahoo, aol/aim, google talk (gtalk), jabber and icq

2. Joopz : Allows users to send text messages from the Web to both individuals and groups, while enabling recipients to respond directly to the originating PC or Mac. Joopz web texts can be sent from any web-enabled device worldwide to any U.S. or Canadian mobile phone.

3. campfire : Simple, Web-based group chat for businesses, Campfire allows real-time sharing, editing, and collaboration for team members in a secure, password-protected chat.

4. Goowy : is a web based application offering free web and flash email service that enables you instant messaging, email, chat and much more

5. Gizmo : Gizmo Project uses your internet connection (broadband or dial-up) to make calls to other computers. With the click of a mouse, you're connected to friends, family, and colleagues anywhere on earth. It's just that simple. You talk clearly. For as long as you want. For free.

6. eBuddy : web based messaging for everyone, everywhere. E-Messenger is a web application that enables you to chat with your MSN, AOL and Yahoo buddies without having to install any program or Java applet.

7. e-messenger : Online messaging from eBuddy is a web messenger application which supports MSN, Yahoo and AIM (AOL). When your school or office has blocked IM you can use the web version of eBuddy with any standard JavaScript enabled browser, even behind a firewall.

8. ILOVEIM : eBuddy is a web messenger application which supports MSN, Yahoo and AIM (AOL). When your school or office has blocked IM you can use the web version of eBuddy with any standard JavaScript enabled browser, even behind a firewall.

Images & Photos

1. Flickr : The best way to stor, search, sort and share your photos

2. Zooomr : Universally the best way to share, search, store and sort your photos online.

3. Slide :

4. zoto

5. 23HQ : Are your photos stuck on your hard drive, instead of being shared with the people who matter to you?

6. Mybloop : MyBloop – sharing pictures, audio, and video for free, whithout storage limits and additional software to install

Blogs

1. Blogger : your easy-to-use web site, where you can quickly post thoughts, interact with people, and more

2. Weblogs, Inc : Creating trade weblogs across niche industries in which user participation is an essential component of the resulting product.

3. BlogCode : BlogCode.com is a fast, easy and intuitive source of blog recommendations based on the StoryCode.com model. It allows you to start with your favourite weblog (or perhaps even your own) and find...

4. blo.gs : lets you keep an eye on your favorite weblogs via the web and email. You can even put the list on your site: a blogroll that knows what is new!

5. BlogLines : a FREE online service for searching, subscribing, creating and sharing news feeds, blogs and rich web content.

Bookmarking

1. Digg : Digg is all about user powered content. Everything is submitted and voted on by the digg community. Share, discover, bookmark, and promote stuff that's important to you!

2. del.icio.us : A social bookmarks manager. Using bookmarklets, you can add bookmarks to your list and categorize them

3. Reddit : Reddit is a source for what's new and popular online. Reddit learns what you like as you vote on existing links or submit your own!

4. StumbleUpon : StumbleUpon uses thumbs up and down ratings to form collaborative opinions on website quality. When you stumble, you will only see pages which friends and like-minded stumblers have liked

5. Blinklist : Real people with shared interests list the websites they care about. Rate sites you like or save them for later.

6. Blummy : A free tool for quick access to your favorite web services via your bookmark toolbar, Blummy lets you add and customize widgets that do practically anything: add pictures to Flickr, submit sites to del.icio.us, look up text in Wikipedia. Choose from hundreds of custom "blummlets" or create your own.

7. Techcrunch : TechCrunch is a blog about Web 2.0 products & companies, many of the posts written by Michael Arrington. The blog's first post was on June 11, 2005

8. Furl : Make your favorite web bookmarks accessible from anywhere with Furl's lightweight bookmarklet. Furl allows you to easily save, take notes on and share the links you've stored, or browse others' most popular bookmarks to find new and interesting things.

9. Spurl : Never lose track of a web site again with

Spurl's free on-line bookmarking service and search engine. Spurl stores addresses quickly for easy access with a one-click bookmarklet and provides recommendations for new content based on your preferences

10. Trailfire : Bookmaking sharing software.

VOIP

1. Jajah : jah is a VoIP (Voice over IP) provider, founded by Austrians Roman Scharf and Daniel Mattes in 2005[1]. The Jajah headquarters are located in Mountain View, CA, USA, and Luxembourg. Jajah maintains a development centre in Israel.

2. skype : It's free to download and free to call other people on Skype. Skype the number one voice over ip software

3. Private Phone : a free local phone number with voicemail and messages you can check online or from any phone.

Games & Sketching

1. Trendio : Trendio.com is an online prediction market. Users, instead of buying stock in companies with real money, buy stock in certain news subjects with fake money. Words available include those from the world of politics, sport, and entertainment. The more the word appears in the news, the higher the value of the stock. Currently, the site uses about 3,000 online internet sources to gauge the value of each word.

2. GameSnips : online games list, digg style. Voting for each game, sort lists by latest or by votes

3. Pictaps : Roxik Pictaps – Draw a Character and Watch It Dance in 3D

4. Broadcast Game : The objective of the Broadcast game is to connect all of the terminals and cables on the grid to the central hub by fixing their orientations. All you need to do is click and rotate the cables, the terminals, or the hub.

5. Pikipimp.com : Ever wanted to add bling to your iomages? Pikpimp is a relly cool ajax application that allows you to drop and drag objects on your image. Save the image and add to your site!

6. Mainada : How aobut Comic Sketch (thanks *Tiago*)

Wikis

1. Wikipedia : The biggest multilingual free-content encyclopedia on the Internet. Over two million articles and still growing.

2. LittleWiki : LittleWiki is a Web site where you can create public and private wiki pages. A Wiki is a Web site where anyone can enter and edit content. That means you can post and edit information about virtually anything you wish, and you can read what others have posted too.

3. Wetpaint : Wetpaint powers websites that tap the power of collaborative thinking. The heart of the Wetpaint advantage is its ability to allow anyone — especially those without technical skill — to create and contribute to websites written for and by those who share a passion or interest. To do this, Wetpaint combines the best aspects of wikis, blogs, forums and social networks so anyone can click and type on the web.

4. JotSpot : Create and share wiki pages with a WYSIWYG editor via Jotspot's secure wiki hosting. Install various "applications" to refine your wiki content – project manager, company directory, blog, forum, poll, calendar, and more – then invite others to contribute

5. PBWiki : Make a free, password protected wiki as easily as a peanut butter sandwich. Easily upload HTML, link files to your pages, integrate RSS, and more.

Office Tools

1. Zoho Office Suite : Online Word Processor

2. Google Docs & Spreadsheets : With Google Docs & Spreadsheets, you can: * Use our online editor to format documents, spell-check and more. * Upload Word documents, OpenOffice, RTF, HTML or text. * Download...

3. Num Sum : Easy, Sharable Web Spreadsheets

4. Dictinary : Online dictionary

5. notifyr.org : Be ahead of the rest with notifyr.org. Notifyr is an easy to use tool which lets anybody easily receive instant updates on any web page around the world. Notifyr.org is ideal for those who want instant information on new stock, or new product release information. Best of all it's free – and always will be

6. ThinkFree Office : Have you ever wanted to edit an Excel spreadsheet on a Linux system? Have you ever wanted to show your colleagues a presentation on a computer not equipped with Powerpoint? Would you like to be able...

7. Numly : Numly is a web 2.0 startup offering next generation copyright and DRM licensing services for ali things digital.

8. gOffice : Free online word processor, utput can be pdf or html letters, allows personalization in letter templates..

RSS

1. FeedBurner : FeedBurner helps bloggers, podcasters and commercial publishers get more value from the content they create. Our advanced feed management technology deftly delivers subscription services for...

2. Feed Digest : Feed Digest is a parser, regenerator, and syndicator for, and of, RSS and Atom feeds. It lets you do things like put the content of RSS or Atom feeds on your own site(s).

3. Attensa : Attensa, Inc. is a venture backed software company developing RSS readers, online RSS aggregators, enterprise RSS servers and RSS infrastructure software that automatically and intelligently delivers...

4. Tiny Tiny RSS : Tiny Tiny RSS is a web-based news feed aggregator, designed to allow you to read news from any location, while feeling as close to a real desktop application as possible.

5. Feed43 : This free online service converts any web page to an RSS feed on the fly.

6. Feed Mailer : feeds direct to your email. (thanks John)

Emails

1. Gmail : Gmail is an experiment in a new kind of webmail, built on the idea that you should never have to delete mail and you should always be able to find the message you want.

2. 30 Gigs : 30Gigs.com is invite-only web-based email that offers, you guessed it, 30 gigabytes of space.

3. Zookoda : is an email marketing application designed specifically for bloggers. Zookoda enables you to send a daily, weekly or monthly summary of your latest blog posts directly into your visitors inbox.

4. Sprout : osted email management for your sales and support email. No IT department required. Mailroom can organize your email and suggest replies to save you time and keep you better in touch with your customers. There is nothing to setup and it takes only a minute to get started

5. Gawab : Offers a web mail service with a number of features. Supports POP/SMTP.

News

1. NewsGator : Read all of your favorite news,

websites and blogs all in one place.

2. newsvine.com : Keep track of breaking news with Newsvine: read "The Wire" for a direct stream of articles from the AP and ESPN, and read "The Vine" for Newsvine user submitted content and columns. Interact with other Newsvine readers by voting for and commenting on news, and write/maintain your own Newsvine column.

3. Gabbr : Gabbr is a community-based social news and blogging network which allows users to save and share their favorite top news headlines and blog posts.

4. wired : News site and magazine, covering technology, culture, business and politics.

5. Clipmarks : Bite-size hiligh-lights on the web.

File Sharing

1. Box.Net : Free online file storage and sharing from Box.net! Our internet storage service enables you to save, browse, share, & retrieve files, photos, and documents ...

2. AllPeers : Unleash your online experience and discover unlimited private sharing. Share private photos worry-free. No passwords to remember, no public access. Share your videos without uploading – save on hosting costs while saving time.No cumbersome interface. No sharing restriction. Private and secure. No spyware, no adware, no annoying advertisements.

3. MailBigFile internet application for file sharing

Others

1. Live : Microsoft web 2.0 portal

2. LinkedIn : is like Facebook for business professionals: Build yourself a business network to give you credibility in job searches and hiring, or use LinkedIn to reconnect or keep in touch with important business connections.

3. BaseCamp : Simple project management with to-do lists, milestones, time tracking, file sharing, calendars, and more. Basecamp is a solution for taking charge of communication, collaboration, and organization for projects big and small.

4. Side Job Track : A job tracking application for independent contractors, Sidejobtrack creates and manages invoices for goods, services, and time, then produces monetary reports to track payments and income.

5. Kayak.com searches hundreds of travel sites to give you the widest possible choice of flights and prices. It costs nothing to search and not a cent to book because we're not a travel agency.

6. TravBuddy is a site for people who love to explore. You don't have to be traveling across the world to use this site. Maybe you just want to share advice about a local restaurant you enjoy, or perhaps last weekend you discovered an amazing new place to watch the sunset, right in your hometown. Whether you are exploring at home or exploring abroad, the art and joy of discovery is still the same. Something that is familiar to you might be amazing and new to someone who is visiting.

7. Wayfaring is an interesting new site that lets you tag and create your own routes and places on Google maps

8. Omnidrive : As the world's first complete storage aggregator, Omnidrive allows you to bring all your files and content together from your desktop, devices and the web onto a single space that's easily accessible from any platform.

9. ma.gnolia : Build your web site and build community online

10. Ajaxian : Ajax related blog

11. Web 2.0 Sites : web 2.0 sites directory, for all web 2.0 related services.

CONCLUSION

The society is changing drastically. The way of interactions of human being with his surroundings is also changing. The isolated way of study for enhancing level of knowledge is an obsolete means today. Today's society is growing very rapidly and spreading her branches in all possible orientations and thus going to be more and more networked. To sustain in this society one to be more networked. The visibility of one's contribution and/or talent in this networked society is a prime factor for his sustenance and upgrading. It is impossible to acquire potential visibility until and unless we become more and more networked. The traditional knowledge classification system was developed to fulfill the need of the traditional education and library systems. The number of subjects was limited at that time. But with the growth of knowledge, we are facing information explosion and consequently, proliferation of subjects. The traditional hierarchy of division of knowledge can't fulfill all information needs of today's society. Capacity of reading and thinking was the pillar of success in earlier days. The wisdom was the base of the success. But today's pillar of success stands on the skill of tracing out right bit of information at right time. Information seeking capacity is the base of today's success. The traditional information management systems are thus gradually being outmoded. Then what's the way out? How the spectrum of knowledge could be remodeled to develop a new system of knowledge classification? The new concepts of co-operative tagging or folksonomy, domain ontology, semantic web – are all appearing with some possible solutions restricted to a limited area with a limited context. An overall, integrated solution is yet to come in the picture. Continuous feasibility studies of these new concepts on different areas of interests and with varying contexts to test their suitable applicabilities are acutely necessary now. Different case studies with these new concepts with different user groups will possibly bring some integrated solution for the future. Since information science is highly empirical in nature, therefore multiple investigations through a potential number of cases only may bring any new theory with a new shape.

References

Bliss, Henry E. *A system of bibliographic classification.* New York: H. W. Wilson, 1935.

Broughton, V., Hansson, J., Hjørland, B., & López-Huertas, M. J. (2005). Knowledge organization.

Cutter, Charles A. Common Sense in Libraries. In Charles Ammi Cutter: Library, 1889.

Cutter, Charles A. Rules for a Dictionary Catalog. W.P. Cutter, ed. 4th ed. Washington: Government Printing Office. 1904. (Repr. London: The Library Association, 1962.)

Denning, P.J. Electronic Junk, Communications of the ACM no. 23 vol. 3, 1982.

Dutta, B. An analytical investigation into the characteristics of a subject: A case study. Thesis submitted in the Department of Library and Information Science, Jadavpur University, Kolkata in 2008.

Fichter, D. Intranet applications for tagging and folksonomies. *Online,* 30(3), 2006, pp 43-45.

Golder, S. A., & Huberman, B. A. Usage patterns of collaborative tagging systems. Journal of Information Science, 32(2), 2006. pp 198-208.

Guarino, Nicola. Formal ontology, conceptual analysis and knowledge representation. International Journal of

Human Computer Studies 43(5-6), 1995. pp 625-640.

Guy, M., & Tonkin, E. Tidying up tags? *D-Lib Magazine,* 12(1), 2006. (Retrieved from http://www.dlib.org/dlib/january06/guy/01guy.html)

Herring, C. Distill or drown: the need for reviews. *Physics Today* 21 (9): 1968, 27-33.

Hiltz, S.R. and Turoff, M. Structuring Computer-mediated Communication Systems to avoid Information Overload. Communications of the ACM, Vol. 28 No 7 July 1985, pp 680-689.

Kroski, E. The hive mind: Folksonomies and user-based tagging, 2006. (http://infotangle.blogsome.com/2005/12/07/the-hive-mind-folksonomies-and-user-based-tagging/)

Malone et al: Intelligent Information-sharing systems. Communications of the ACM, Vol. 30, No. 5, 1987, pp 390-402.

Maness. J. Library 2.0 Theory: Web 2.0 and its implications for libraries. Webology. 3(2), 2006.

Mathes, A. Folksonomies - cooperative classification and communication through shared metadata, 2004. Retrieved from http://www.adammathes.com/academic/computer-mediated-communication/folksonomies.html

Mitchell, R. L. Tag teams wrestle with web content. Computerworld, 38(16), 2005, p. 31.

Palme, J. You have 134 Unread Mail! Do You Want To Read Them Now? by Jacob Palme. In Proceedings of the IFIP Wg 6.5 Working Conference on Computer-Based Message Services, 1984.

Quintarelli, E. Folksonomies: Power to the people. 2005. (http://www.iskoi.org/doc/folksonomies.htm)

Ranganathan, S.R. Prolegomena to library classification. Ed. 3. London: Asia Publ. House, 1967.

Richardson, E. C. Classification: Theoretical and Practical. 3.ed. New York: H. W. Wilson, 1930.

Sayers, W. C. *Canons for Classification.* London: Grafton, 1915.

Shirky, C. Folksonomy. 2004. (http://www.corante.com/many/archives/2004/08/25/folksonomy.php)

Systematizer, ed. Francis L. Miksa, 99-105. Littleton: Libraries Unlimited, Inc. 1977.

Taylor, Arlene G. The Organization of Information. Westport: Libraries Unlimited, 2004.